Move Forward

Powerful Strategies for Creating Better Outcomes in Life

Bill Bodri

Top Shape Publishing, LLC
1135 Terminal Way Suite 209
Reno, NV 89502

ISBN-10: 0972190775
ISBN-13: 978-0-9721907-7-0
Library of Congress Number: 2016917179

DEDICATION

Many people want to change their life in a significant way, but don't know how to do it or are afraid to start making any efforts. They need to know that there *is* such a thing as cause and effect which controls your life. The outcome of the present circumstances you can control is created by your habits, thoughts and beliefs that turn into actions or non-actions. If you can properly change your thoughts and actions to go against an unfortunate, unwholesome or unwelcome "groove" that is pulling you like a magnet, then you can certainly change your situation and finally move forward to a better life. For those who have decided to make the effort, this book is dedicated to helping you move ahead.

TABLE OF CONTENTS

	Acknowledgments	i
1	Caesar Crosses the Rubicon	1
2	Liao Fan Changes His Fated Fortune	4
3	Ben Franklin Transforms His Unwelcome Personality	18
4	Frank Bettger Discovers the Secret to Business Success	28
5	Develop New Skills Through Deep Deliberate Practice	32
6	Defy Your Genetic Programming	38
7	Attain Spiritual Progress Where None Was Thought Possible	47
8	The Compounding Effect From Maintaining Consistent Effort	75
	Appendix 1: The Story of Shao Kangjie	78
	Appendix 2: Using Blood Test "Optimal Reference Ranges" to Pick Your Nutritional Supplements	82

ACKNOWLEDGMENTS

Whenever I write a book, I always try to "pack it full of meat," meaning that I try to fill it with as many useful, practical things as possible to help your life. This density of content usually provides many more takeaways than in ordinary books, but it also requires extensive editing. I would like to thank Marshall Adair for that difficult task, and John Newtson for helping me come up with a title for this work on self-improvement. We were originally going to call it "Toss the Dice High" to capture Caesar's decision to cross the Rubicon and make his best efforts at capturing Rome, even if he might not succeed, for in life you have to summon up the necessary courage and confidence to make the effort to *Move Forward*. I'm hoping you will find the materials within can help you change your life in new directions you might want, and that you decide to risk making those efforts even though success is never assured. That's the meaning of toss the dice high, which is that despite no assurances you have to risk moving forward to change your fate, fortune and destiny.

Chapter 1
CAESAR CROSSES THE RUBICON

Julius Caesar become Emperor of Rome after struggling through great obstacles and challenges. The pivotal moment on his road to becoming Emperor was when he stood with his troops on the upper banks of the River Rubicon, the northernmost border of Roman territory in Italy.

Caesar had been recalled to Rome by the Senate and knew that once he returned he was certain to be killed. Roman law forbade a general to march on Rome with his army, which would have protected him. Roman law also required him to law down his command if he crossed the Rubicon. He had to surrender his right to order troops and disband with any weapons.

Caesar considered his options. If he marched with his army towards Rome, defying its laws, he would instantly become an outlaw, a public enemy. He would be starting a civil war because he would have to fight his way back to the capital, and he would have to win that war or die. If he disbanded his army and entered alone he also would most certainly be killed.

Caesar paused a moment at the Rubicon and then declared with a loud voice to all those present, "Toss The Dice High." He ordered his troops to move forward, cross the waters and he eventually won Rome.

The rest of the story is great history.

Now some say that Caesar's words should be translated as "the die is cast," meaning that it was now fated that he must fight. This translation unfortunately also suggests that the outcome of the fighting was also fated whereas at that moment in time the final outcome could not be known. The only "fated outcome" at that moment was that Caesar must now fight and struggle to win or be killed.

Some translate Caesar's words as "roll the dice" or "let the game be ventured" with the gambling connotation that luck would decide the outcome. However, Caesar was not tossing his luck to fate but became determined to create an outcome he hoped to win through effort. "Toss the dice high" actually means, "There is no turning back. I will cross the river and we will see what comes out of my best efforts. I will be fighting a war, and I will do everything to ensure I am the winner."

After you throw dice and they start rolling they cannot be controlled. Similarly, in life you can only control your actions, but not the results of those actions. Because risk is always present, in life you must therefore determine if the goals you seek are worthy of your efforts. Are those goals truly worthy of your time, money and life force? If so, then cross the Rubicon and start taking the action steps you must take to move ahead.

Caesar showed that positive action is required for moving forward to create a new fortune and destiny. If you seize the moment and move with skill you can forge a new fate, but if you just let events occur without lifting a finger then you will always be the unwilling recipient of whatever fortune deals you.

There is no fate in life other than that which you

ultimately create yourself, so I encourage you to make the efforts to get what you want even if you must sail against the wind. You must use your wisdom, smart actions and gritty perseverance to get to the destination you desire.

Therefore, don't just gamble or toss the result up to luck but try to actively create that specific fortune you desire. No results are assured in life, so the only question to ask is whether the venture is worth the commitment of your risking. Is it worth spending your life force on this goal? Is it worth your efforts?

Before you are yet many years more of life left to be lived so you, too, face a decision as important as Caesar's. You can let the winds of fate blow you this way or that, or you can choose to start sailing to a new destination you want with the understanding that you will have to tack, jib and haul to get to that final location.

My advice is to seize the day! Commit to a life of change even though it will involve effort and take you out of your comfort zone. There is no reward without risk so step up to confidence and *venture the risk* since the outcome is something you truly want in your life.

With wise effort you can change your fate and fortune.

With wise effort you can change your personality.

With wise effort you can learn new skills and talents you thought impossible to master.

With wise effort you can eliminate disease, become healthier and even defy your genetic propensities.

With wise effort you may not necessarily be able to create a perfect life, but will come closer to shaping the ideal life you desire.

Move forward, move ahead by taking the steps necessary to change your life.

Chapter 2
LIAO FAN CHANGES
HIS FATED FORTUNE

For those who believe in karma, there is a famous eastern tale of spirituality, rooted in Buddhism and Confucianism, that teaches people how to change their fate, fortune and destiny. You can find the entire story in the book *Liao Fan's Four Lessons*, written by Yuan Liao Fan.

The story goes that during China's Ming dynasty (in the 1500s), an ordinary man named Yuan Liao Fan started to study medicine to become a doctor. His mother had persuaded him to study the healing arts instead of studying to pass the imperial civil service examinations because it would be a good way for him to support himself while helping others.

During a chance meeting during a meditation retreat, Liao Fan met an elderly fortune teller named Kong who told Liao Fan that he shouldn't be studying medicine because he was destined to become a government official. During that time all government positions were attained by passing the special imperial exams, and Kong asked him, "Why aren't you studying for the government examinations?"

It was surprising to Liao Fan that a perfect stranger could know anything about his life and fate to make such a suggestion. Liao Fan and his mother initially didn't believe Kong and his forecasting abilities, but decided to test him on all sorts of predictions. Using the strange method of Iron Abacus Numerology developed by the sage Shao Kangjie, which calculates out the index numbers of sentences in a special book that reveals your fated fortune, they found that Kong's predictions on all sorts of matters, great and small, were always accurate.

As a result, Liao Fan started studying for the imperial exams as Kong had recommended. Kong said he would pass with the rank of 14th place in the county exam, 71st in the regional exam and 9th in the provisional exam; and Liao Fan passed the examinations exactly as predicted.

Kong then calculated predictions for the rest of Liao Fan's life including all the years he would pass civil service exams and in what location, the years he would attain various government promotions, what they would be, and so on. The Iron Abacus Numerology method had revealed that his final appointment in life would be as a magistrate in Sichuan province serving for three and a half years, after which he would retire, return home and die at age fifty-three on a particular date without any heirs.

Being a well educated man, Liao Fan continued to view those predictions with skepticism, but everything happened exactly as predicted for five consecutive years. There was even an amazing prediction that he would be promoted after receiving a ration of 259 bushels of rice. He was actually recommended for a promotion after receiving only 200 bushels, so he started to doubt the prediction. However, a new boss turned down the recommendation. Some time later a new commissioner promoted him after reviewing his case and he got his new post after receiving exactly the amount of rice that had been calculated. Kong's amazing predictions had proved to be one hundred percent accurate, and from that point on Liao Fan deeply believed that everything in life was fated. Everything, he felt, happened in due time according to fate, including the length of one's life span.

Hinduism, Jainism, Yoga, Taoism, Buddhism and many other eastern spiritual schools certainly believe in karma, and that you come into this world with a life span that is fated. As the length of your life is fated, so they say that the number of your breaths is fated as well. However, they also teach that hard work and merit can change this predetermined amount. In other words, you can change your fate and fortune.

According to the karmic principles of causality, the merit you bring with you when you are born is fixed unless you work throughout life to increase it or replenish it. If you squander your merit in foolish activities then you will simply waste life without accomplishing anything new at all. If you cultivate a kind mind of charity and giving, however, then because there is no limit to your mind at the moment of giving then the rewards you receive in response can be equally as great as that expanse. *In other words, what you achieve in life will all depend on your mindset and efforts.*

Liao Fan, however, started to believe that health and sickness, life and death, marriage and divorce, wealth and poverty and all other aspects of life were perfectly fixed. Believing in fate and predestination, he began to view everything in a detached manner and ceased to seek gain or profit or any special achievements out of the ordinary.

Liao Fan was eventually selected as an imperial student, and was sent to the University of Beijing to study for one year where he began the practice of meditation in earnest. With practice he achieved some progress where he could sit with his mind in silence.

Afterwards he went to Nanjing for one year where he happened to attend a meditation retreat with Zen Master Yungu. Master Yungu saw him meditate for three days and nights without much sleep and asked him why he had become so excellent at sitting without any wandering thoughts or mental attachments. Master Yungu said, "The reason why ordinary people cannot become enlightened is because they hold to meandering thoughts. In our three-day meditation I have not observed you succumb to any such wandering thoughts. Why is that?"

Liao Fan replied, "The entire outcome of my life has been accurately predicted and the timing of everything is predestined. Everything such as promotion or failure and even life and death are fated so there is no need for me to desire any goals. I already know how everything will unfold. Because of fate there is no room for other results than what is already fated so there is no need for me to desire anything. It is useless to even think about it, so it is easy for my mind to become naturally settled."

Master Yungu then slapped him with the words, "I thought you were someone of special capability because you were able to sit (meditate) well with very few meandering thoughts, but now I see from your answer that you are no more than a common person."

The Zen master explained that most people are entirely subject to fate. They merely chase after external achievements without turning inwards to cultivate their minds, and so they are bound to their karma. At most they only attain in life what fate has already entitled them to achieve and enjoy. Even an extraordinarily talented person is still bound by their prior destiny when they don't bother to cultivate their freedom from old habits, patterns of behavior and attachments.

A person's fate is truly created by his own past thoughts and deeds just as the returns you receive in life are indeed the fruit of your karma. If someone attains one million dollars in this life it is because they have cultivated the good fortune worthy of that amount.

Therefore if you want to achieve more than what you already have in store then you have to act in such a way that *your destiny will be re-created*. Positive efforts can slowly carve out a new reward that modifies fate and creates a new pattern of destiny. You must simply take charge of the process. You must detach from the karmic thoughts and propensities that carve out a predestined fate and go against his grain of those energies to create a new future. Only meditation can teach you how to disassociate from or ignore the thoughts that would normally control you along a destined causeway.

"You can live life as though everything is predestined and fated," Zen master Yungu explained, "using up whatever stores you have in your karmic merit bank until it is empty and your life ends, or you can cultivate good thoughts and do good deeds to replenish your merits and move ahead. By so doing you will accumulate positive karma and this merit will result in magnifying your life and the lives of those around you.

"If you want to change your fortune you should not give in to wandering thoughts. Then you will most easily receive a response. Only a mind empty of wandering thoughts that jump from here to there can transcend the predetermination of mathematics. Otherwise an individual will tend to be bound by destiny.

"When your mind reaches a stage of emptiness, or non-attachment, that is where you will be able to create a new fortune and destiny since within the formlessness of non-attachment to what arises there is as yet no set pattern. You are not attaching to your old karmic thought patterns when you practice the formlessness of detachment. When our spiritual cultivation and self-cultivation reaches a certain level of mental excellence in this respect then our destiny will certainly change. The change will depend upon your accumulation of merits and upon seeking a response (help) from (the beings in) Heaven."

"Furthermore," Yungu said, "destiny simply cannot control those who have accomplished numerous exemplary deeds. For twenty years you have been bound by Mr. Kong's predictions and done nothing to change them, so you are just an ordinary person. Since you have not cultivated extremely good deeds then your life has accorded with exactly what had been predicted. If you subject yourself to a disciplined course of action that moves you forward despite your old thought patterns that hold you back in your old predestined fortune, then you can attain whatever you seek by re-creating your destiny rather than being constrained by a fortune."

Liao Fan listened respectfully to Master Yungu but objected, saying that fame, wealth and prestige might be attainable through seeking, but their seeking and attainment were probably already predestined. Therefore, non-attainment or failure was also probably fated regardless of any efforts we made.

This makes some sense, because according to karmic theory the desire for most things arises from previous lives. Therefore one would exert great effort to attain those desires as the materialization of that karma. (In other words, your efforts and their outcome are both already karmically fated.) If you choose to seek something that you were not supposed to have, in that case the seeking would be useless, but it would still be karma that caused you to make the fruitless effort.

This is what Liao Fan argued: if you are not supposed to have something, then regardless of how hard you seek you will not get it.

Referencing the teachings of the Zen school and Confucianism, Master Yungu explained that everything starts from the mind and everything is experienced within consciousness. If we were to seek first from within the mind and build an outcome there, then starting from the inner we will have an actual chance to build a fortune in the outer world that is not already predestined. The mind is by nature empty, and if we build from its foundations of formlessness then we can bring something new into the real world.

All seeking must start from the mind, which is an instrument subject to changes. If we could stay continually concentrated with our thoughts along a proper course or reach a state where thoughts were entirely absent, we would create an opportunity where fate would no longer bind us and we could actively create a new fortune.

Yes, you can seek and attain something not destined in your life, but such a goal requires that you become an active, disciplined doer. You need to pursue the goal with grit and perseverance and ignore wandering thoughts that sidetrack you from your goals. You must avoid being someone whose motivation sways and who ends up following directionless meandering thoughts. The jumpy monkey's mind we harbor that leaps from place to place lacks the concentration necessary to produce high outcomes in life. Instead of allowing your own mind to harbor scattered thoughts like a monkey's, you must become a channeled thinker and doer.

This is an approach that is utterly practical and scientific.

After having convinced Liao Fan that he needed to change his ways, Master Yungu then introduced him to a the method of keeping a ledger of merits and demerits - a daily ledger for recording his good deeds *and* faults - so that he might track his efforts at changing his fortune. This was designed to help Liao Fan work on polishing his mind and promote inner qualities such as virtue, honesty, integrity, mercy and kindness. He had to start becoming less selfish and perform more charitable deeds since this would, by the laws of karma, create a new stock of merit which he could spend, like money, on achieving the results he wanted.

In the system Yungu recommended, Liao Fan was to record both his good and bad deeds (including thoughts) for each day in order to learn how to govern his behavior and his mind. One good deed cancelled out one bad deed and the net result for each day would be either positive or negative. These were recorded and the accumulation of the results showed him if he was making progress at changing himself or not.

Liao Fan was also taught to recite a mantra requesting help from heaven in his efforts. He was taught that it would help him watch his mind, correct his behavior, do good deeds and create opportunities for changing his fortune as desired.

Upon receiving this lesson, Liao Fan regretted his incorrect notions. He looked carefully at his life, taking stock of his errant habits and behaviors, and acknowledged that they had prevented him from getting ahead and were responsible for a large portion of his bad fortune. Overall, he recognized how his character faults of being harsh, impatient, intolerant, self-indulgent, quick-tempered and undisciplined had contributed to his inability to progress as much as he wanted in life. Liao Fan also had to admit that he drank too much and at night stayed up too late, which harmed his vital energy.

Additionally, Liao Fan recognized that he lacked loving-kindness and would not sacrifice anything for others; and that this was a serious character fault. He also recognized that he was doing little or nothing to benefit society and help those who were suffering. He was too fond of gossip and liked criticizing others. He often spoke angrily without restraint which ended in quarrels and destroyed various chances. He was impatient and narrow-minded in not being able to accept others. He would show off his intelligence and abilities by putting others down, thus creating bad feelings and destroying relationships. He was not working towards accumulating any of the virtues that would build up a stock of good merit and help him go against fortune to get promoted beyond his calculated fate.

Liao Fan sincerely regretted his faults and ways of doing things. This sincere regret and his vow to personally change then became the key to changing his destiny. As you probably know, you must become aware of your mistakes before you can correct them and Liao Fan finally saw his errors for what they were. Like clearing a garden of weeds so that the crops can grow unencumbered, you should work at eliminating personal faults that stand in the way of a better future just as you must work at eliminating obstacles (or transcending challenges) that block any road of achievement you are on.

Master Yungu had stated, "After you recognize your shortcomings, you need to *do all you can to change* and correct your misdeeds that have prevented you from attaining any fortune you are after. To correct faults is to improve in your self-cultivation."

Liao Fan determined that he would change his fortune. He would make the effort. He would try to move ahead. He would change his destiny through a positive push and would follow Master Yungu's teachings to do so.

Master Yungu had taught him that a person had to change himself in order to change his fortune, and also needed to perform good deeds and practice virtuous behaviors to do so. In front of a Buddha statue, Liao Fan then vowed to reform his ways (cultivate to change himself) and pledged 3,000 good deeds if Heaven would help him pass a higher imperial exam than what was fated.

Amazingly, fortune teller Kong's predictions, that had so far been accurate down to the tiniest detail, then started to lose their accuracy. Thus, in the next preliminary imperial exam Liao Fan took 1st place where he was supposed to take 3rd place, and in the Autumn he passed an exam which Kong predicted would not be possible. This is what you can also expect for yourself if, like Caesar, you determine what you must do to change your fate and with an unwavering mind set out to achieve it; and if, like Liao Fan you undertake in a discipline fashion to change yourself and your behavior in the process.

After ten years of constant effort, Liao Fan's 3,000 good deeds were finally accumulated as he had vowed and he respectfully dedicated them at a temple, demonstrating both his respect and thanks to Heaven for its assistance. Similarly, some people examine their daily tally of merits and demerits in the evening just before bed and ritualistically dedicate their efforts (at change and accomplishment) to Heaven at that time.

Inspired by these successes, Liao Fan continued his cultivation. Because he wished for a son, which was not included in his fortune, Liao Fan vowed to perform another 3,000 good deeds which together with his wife he accumulated in four year's time. Against fate they finally received a child they had hoped for – their son Yuan Tian Chi.

Liao Fan then vowed to perform 10,000 more good deeds if Heaven could help him pass a yet higher imperial examination degree, and after three years he succeeded and promoted to become mayor of the city of Baodi. These passing marks and his subsequent appointment were also in excess of his predicted fate.

In his new position Liao Fan did not have as many opportunities as previously to perform good deeds and worried that he could not complete his vow. However, one night he dreamed that lowering the taxes for the county was equivalent to 10,000 good deeds, but he did not trust this type of thinking. Doubting that this could produce such great merit, he asked a visiting Zen master who told him, "A single kind deed done with a pure heart can be worth that much or more. Since 10,000 people are going to benefit if you lower the taxes, of course this would earn you great merit."

Liao Fan originally had the fortune that he would die at age fifty-three without a male heir, but he begat a son, lived two decades or more beyond his allotted time span, and achieved a position far higher than what fate had originally intended. He wrote his entire story in *Liao Fan's Four Lessons*, which I often recommend to others, detailing how he changed his fortune and destiny.

Liao Fan explained that fortune and destiny definitely

exist, as does karma, but this is not widely believed because it is hard for people to trace an outcome or event to its original sources. Furthermore, fate, fortune and karma are changeable but the power to change them comes from you because they ultimately originate from yourself. You are the one who created them so you also have the power to change them.

As long as you are willing to reform the habits that distract you from the outcome you seek, apply yourself with determination (along a wise and skillful road of achievement), practice kind words, deeds and thoughts to accumulate virtue and merits, then there is nothing that you cannot achieve. Your own efforts to create good fortune will bear personal fruit that no one can take away from you. You can then use those merits for positive accomplishments.

The ancient sages who revealed the rules of astrology and fortune telling taught that while there is such a thing as fate, we can also certainly change it - otherwise there would be no point to knowing it. If everything was predestined, what would be the point of astrology and systems like Iron Abacus Numerology or the *I-Ching* that teach us how to guide the changes of life to bring about what we seek?

You can actively transform your fate into a new fortune that defies destiny rather than be bound by it. Liao Fan's story shows us how:

First, practice meditation to increase your powers of self-awareness. Through careful introspection, determine what faults, errors or habits are obstacles to achieving the fortune you seek and start working to cut them off. The Immortal Li Qingyun said, "Don't be afraid of having thoughts. Just be afraid of not being aware of your thoughts that arise. Having wicked (non-virtuous) or wrong thoughts is a sickness. Stopping them is the cure. Once errant thoughts are stopped, they will be cured and other wicked thoughts won't arise."

By eliminating faults and errant thought habits that stand in the way of achieving a particular fortune, we thereby pave the way for its achievement because the obstacles preventing it are eliminated. Even if you don't achieve the new fate you want, eliminating faults through mindfulness and self-awareness is like cutting and polishing a diamond where the practice itself has the reward of self-perfection.

Increased awareness also enables you to see opportunities to make progress along your personal path and do more good in the world. Doing good deeds may seem tangential from, or separate from the actions you need to get ahead, and yet they often create positive circumstances that might mysteriously help you in accomplishing your goals. In inexplicable ways they can create the merit necessary for you to strike out on a new road of achievement.

Second, once you decide to embark upon a new road of change and achievement you will need to establish a system to help you maintain that initial drive and motivating spark of ignition. Liao Fan's ledger book of merits and demerits for recording your daily efforts will be very effective in helping you to maintain your motivation to keep progressing. This type of daily journal will serve as the means to keep you on course and always moving forward. It is like a compass that maintains your direction and like a motor that powers your movement.

Third, ask for help from Heaven in your efforts. In the west people commonly recite daily prayers asking for Heaven's watchful eyes and blessings. In Liao Fan's case he daily recited the powerful Zhunti mantra of Buddhism (Namah saptanam samyak sambuddha kotinam tadyatha om cale cule cundi svaha),[1] which is known for helping people change their fortunes. From India and China come

---

[1] The last half of the mantra is pronounced "Om Zherli Zhewli Zhunti Soha."

many types of mantras that request help from higher powers (spiritual beings) to assist us in changing our fortunes, such as Mahakala or Kubera for wealth matters, Manjushri and Saraswati for wisdom matters, Shiva and Buddha for enlightenment, or Bhaisajyaguru (the "Medicine Buddha") for sickness.

The choice whether to seek good fortune or bring about adversity, to create a new life or simply accept what fate brings you, the choice whether to create a particular outcome or drift along with whatever comes is all up to you.

The *Yoga Vasistha* of ancient India says that what we call fate or divine will is nothing other than the result of our efforts of the past, but our present actions have infinitely more power and potential than the past in changing this. Our present actions have the power to change any karma that is already fated. Setting out to change a "fixed" result will doubtless encounter friction, however, so one must throw away wandering thoughts on such a path, cultivation grit and concentration, and devotedly keep to a course of action that will capture the desired outcome.

Indian culture says that if you see that the present self-effort towards a goal is sometimes thwarted by what people call fate, keep on striving because it just means that your current efforts are weak. A man's actions indeed move along the lines that his own karma traces for him, but he is also free to fashion new karma as well that can be experienced in this life. It is there for the choosing. As Caesar showed, determinism exists only to the extent that we do not make an effort. A weak willed man simply gives up and does nothing to change his circumstances, ignorantly attributing everything that happens to God (rather than his personal karma) when it is really up to him and his efforts to carve out a new fortune.

Those people who are satisfied with their fate, who believe change is impossible, or who are satisfied with the fruits of their past efforts will never have the motivation for self-efforts. It is necessary to make a constant effort to move forward to an uncharted future, and you will doubtless encounter difficulties and obstacles. But you cannot stop if you really want a new fortune. You must persevere to move ahead. If you are not ready to stand the course, if you don't use a method that keeps you fused to forward progress, then you are unlikely to move forwards despite your best wishes, hopes and intentions.

In short, destiny, fate, and fortune do exist but can be changed through proper cultivation. You are the force that brings good fortune or adversity yourself, and it is possible to change your fortune by *taking material steps and spiritually significant action.*

First, make the resolution to change and reform your behavior. Second, chart a course of actions to undertake and a way to monitor your efforts so that the feedback helps you stay on track. Third, begin the efforts.

Chapter 3
BEN FRANKLIN TRANSFORMS HIS UNWELCOME PERSONALITY

Most school children know something about the life of Benjamin Franklin. They think of him as a famous printer and call him the man who "discovered electricity," but Franklin was much, much more.

In addition to being a postmaster, newspaper editor and printer he was the author of *Poor Richard's Almanack*. He was also a soldier, statesman, diplomat, philosopher, scientist and inventor (bifocal glasses, glass harmonica, lightning rods, Franklin stove and urinary catheter).

Franklin co-founded the first American hospital, the first subscription library and the American Philosophical Society. He pioneered (and was the first President of) what eventually became the University of Pennsylvania. He also started a police force, a fire company and street lighting in Philadelphia. He accomplished all this despite only having two years of formal education.

Benjamin Franklin was also the only individual to sign all four founding documents of the United States of America – the Declaration of Independence, the Articles of Confederation, U.S. Constitution and Bill of Rights. He had also shaped the Albany Plan of Union.

Frankly, Franklin was the most accomplished American of his time, and many foreign countries (France, England, etcetera) saw him as the archetypal American. He left an outstanding legacy in science, literature and political achievements that has rarely been matched. Truthfully, Franklin's many efforts and activities helped to establish the shape of America. Of all the men who made independence possible for America, probably none mattered more than Franklin and only George Washington mattered as much. When he died, an incredible twenty thousand Philadelphians – nearly half the city – turned out for his funeral.

This wonderful resume begs the question as to how Franklin became this way? The situation is even more perplexing when you discover that Franklin was extremely argumentative and disliked in his youth. He was so disliked that when individuals saw him coming they would cross to the other side of the street to avoid having to greet him and engage in polite conversation.

Recognizing that he had some terrible character flaws, Franklin conceived the idea of changing his personality and behavior, hoping that by cultivating certain virtues this would change his life.

He wrote in his biography,

It was about this time that I conceiv'd the bold and arduous Project of arriving at moral Perfection. I wish'd to live without committing any Fault at any time; I would conquer all that either Natural Inclination, Custom, or Company might lead me into. As I knew, or thought I knew, what was right and wrong, I did not see why I might not *always* do the one and avoid the other. But I soon found I had undertaken a Task of more Difficulty than I had imagined. While my

Attention was taken up in guarding against one Fault, I was often surpris'd by another. Habit took the Advantage of Inattention. Inclination was sometimes too strong for Reason. I concluded at length, that the mere speculative Conviction that it was our Interest to be completely virtuous, was not sufficient to prevent our Slipping, and that the contrary Habits must be broken and good ones acquired and established, before we can have any Dependence on a steady uniform Rectitude of Conduct.[2]

We all know that the motivation to perform some deed or accomplish some grand objective may be strong at first, but the initial urge and spark of interest usually wanes over time, especially after encountering hardships and hindrances. Understanding this, Franklin decided that his overall task of self-perfection was too much to go after all at once. Therefore, he would restrict himself to just thirteen virtues that he wished to cultivate, virtues which would correct what he saw as the main errors in his behavior.

Determining what faults he must correct is something we also saw that Liao Fan did after a bit of honest soul searching.

Most people don't know that Aristotle believed virtue, which he defined as control of the appetites by reason, is a kind of habit. Aristotle said that a man should learn what kind of behavior is good for him and then develop good habits to practice it (much as athletes practice certain ways or movements for their sport). This is exactly what Franklin now intended.

Thinking about what might correct his character faults and be most beneficial to his life, Franklin decided that he

---

[2] Benjamin Franklin, *The Autobiography and Other Writings* (New York: Penguin Books, 1986), pp. 90-91.

should cultivate the virtues of temperance, silence, order, resolution, frugality, industry, sincerity, justice, moderation, tranquility, cleanliness, chastity, and humility. These were the virtues he believed would help him become the man he wanted to be and whose adoption would elevate his life, make him a friendlier character and help him build a more prosperous future. They would make him a better person.

Once he had his mental list of personal faults to be corrected and virtues to be cultivated, Franklin had to create some way in which he would succeed at the task of self-improvement. It is easy to forget our initial inspiration and motivation, and the task of continually working to change one's personality and behavior is hard. Franklin recognized that he therefore needed some type of monitoring system to keep him marching forward at his self-cultivation. He had to police himself constantly to cultivate these virtues; so here is what he did.

Although he wanted to make a habit of all these virtues, it was simply too much to try to pursue them all simultaneously. The pursuit of one would distract his attention from the pursuit of another with the end result that he wouldn't accomplish anything at all if he tried to adopt all of them simultaneously. He therefore decided to pursue each of them in sequence - one at a time.

Franklin decided to devote a week's strictest attention to just one of the character virtues that he wanted to cultivate. After that week he would move to the next perfection on his list, and recognizing that the acquisition of some might help facilitate the acquisition of others he arranged them with this in mind.

Franklin then made a little book in which he dedicated a page to each week in sequence where each new week would represent a concentrated focus on cultivating a specific virtue. He drew seven columns in red ink, one for each day of the week, and each column was marked with a letter for the day such as M (Monday), T (Tuesday), W (Wednesday) and so forth. This is something you could easily do with Microsoft Excel.

He crossed the columns with thirteen rows, each of which was marked with one of the virtues he intended to acquire. Now that he had all these columns and rows, he used a black spot to mark "every Fault I found upon Examination to have been committed respecting that Virtue upon the day."

Each week, Benjamin Franklin would be on his guard, always watching his mind and behavior to avoid going against the major "virtue of the week" while giving the other virtues their normal play. In other words, he put most of his focus on cultivating one specific virtue per week from the lineup. Franklin explained,

> I determined to give a week's strict Attention to each of the Virtues successively. Thus in the first week, my great guard was to avoid every the least offence against *Temperance*, leaving the other virtues to their ordinary chance, only marking every evening the Faults of the day. Thus, if in the first week I could keep my first line, marked T (for Temperance), cleared of spots, I suppos'd the habit of that virtue so much Strengthened, and its opposite Weakened, that I might venture extending my attention to include the next, and for the following week keep both lines clear of spots. Proceeding thus to the last, I could go through a course complete in Thirteen weeks and Four Courses in a year. And like him who, having a garden to weed, does not attempt to Eradicate all the bad herbs at once, which would exceed his reach and his strength, but works on one of the beds at a time, and, having accomplish'd the first, proceeds to a second, so I should have, I hoped, the encouraging pleasure of Seeing on my pages the Progress I made in Virtue, by Clearing successively my lines of their spots, till in the end,

by a number of courses, I should be happy in viewing a Clean Book, after a Thirteen week's daily Examination.[3]

Every evening Franklin would review the day's activities and tabulate his efforts at self-perfection. By rotating the major virtue of focus each week, a complete course of self-perfection efforts could be completed in thirteen weeks, and four complete courses of his efforts could be completed during a full year.

Franklin commented that the habit of keeping the ledger was at times tiresome and difficult just as one would expect. Who really wants to keep at either record keeping or a course of self- perfection?

Actually it is said that the famous Christian monk John Climacus (author of *The Ladder of Divine Ascent*) did something similar. He carried a small notebook hanging from his belt within which he recorded his negative thoughts and behaviors on a daily basis.

In the 1959 film classic, *The Nun's Story*, Audrey Hepburn and the other nun candidates were lined up and given notebooks after which their Mother Superior said, "For the rest of your lives, you will examine your conscience twice a day and write your reflections in these notebooks." In many convents the sisters continue this practice, examining their behavior daily and recording on paper what goes on within their minds including the thoughts that must be corrected. The idea is to arrive at virtuous purity and self-perfection.

Many great Buddhist Kardampa masters (such as the famous Tibetan Geshe Potowa) also kept track of their thoughts during the day - by putting either white or black (good or bad) pebbles in baskets. At the end of the day they would count them to determine if they had made

---

[3] Benjamin Franklin, *The Autobiography of Benjamin Franklin* (New York: Dover Publications, 1996), p. 67.

progress in self-cultivation, and over time through this technique would make deep changes in their personality and behavior.

As Chinese Confucianism and Taoism explain, not being aware of your thoughts, or discovering them too late, is a fault. Christianity also says that we need to monitor our thoughts and behaviors for infractions against what we know to be right. Harboring wrong thoughts is a kind of mental disease, but if you can catch this type of error right away and stop the wrong thoughts that arise in your mind when you are just beginning to play with them, immediately cutting them off is the same as curing them. This is how to improve both your behavior and outcomes in life.

Although it might seem wearisome or inconvenient to some people, Franklin reported that there were two important benefits of his method that should encourage us all to use this technique ourselves.

First, he had the satisfaction of seeing his errors gradually diminish over time due to the plan's application. Small behavioral faults and infractions readily disappeared, the larger ones were reduced, and Franklin had the satisfaction of seeing virtuous ways become second nature.

Second, when he reached the age of seventy-eight, Franklin said that the process had made him a better and happier man than he otherwise would have been and concluded his autobiography by writing, "I hope, therefore, that some of my descendants may follow the example and reap the benefit."

Considering Franklin's great accomplishments in life and how he was able to cultivate countless friendships and bring together differing groups in a spirit of harmony, his ledgering system is a method that you should also consider adopting in conjunction with Liao Fan's ledger of merits and demerits. It is something you can tabulate each night, making into a ritual a reporting of your efforts at self-improvement to Heaven.

People who want to improve their condition in life often complain that they don't know how to do it. They complain that they want to change their life, but fail to recognize that all fate and fortune starts with our thoughts and behavior. Your character determines your fate and fortune, and this methodology of self-improvement recognizes that fact.

You might object to the idea that character is destiny, and think that Franklin's story over-emphasized the importance of cultivating virtues. However, a similar story can be told of former U.S. Treasury Secretary Robert Rubin.

Rubin spent most of his years working for Goldman Sachs where he eventually became the firm's co-chief. He admitted that in his early years at the firm he was, essentially, a jerk who was "impersonal," "short with people," "abrupt and preemptory" and basically not a nice guy.

One day an older partner had a talk with Rubin and said that he could play a larger role in the firm if he changed his personal ways. The advice affected him so much that Rubin vowed to change himself and did. Rubin "started listening to people better, understanding their problems, and valuing their views. He changed an important element of his personality. If he hadn't, it's unlikely he would have become one of the most respected and admired figures at Goldman and on Wall Street.

"Psychologists might argue that people who do what Rubin did aren't changing their personalities, they're changing their behavior in order to override some part of their personalities. Fine; there's no need to quibble. What matters is that they were not constrained by particular traits."[4]

---

[4] Geoff Colvin, *Talent is Overrated: What Really Separates World-Class Performers from Everybody Else* (New York: Penguin Group, 2008), p. 49.

Rubin's story, like Franklin's, show the importance of changing your character to free yourself of old habit energies and dealing with people on a higher plane. Franklin's ledgering method can help you develop these skills as well as change your personality, and thus your fate, just as Rubin showed was possible in a high powered firm. When one looks at the efforts Franklin made to become the best he could be, and the subsequent roles he took in his life and accomplishments he made, one can only conclude that it is worthy to *roll the dice* and undertake such efforts regardless as to whether or not the outcome is assured. One cannot know how far one will get in life, but as Franklin said the rewards from having accepted the task are definitely worth the effort.

In Liao Fan's method you must watch your mind for errors and faults and immediately cut them off when noticed. For instance, if you find yourself getting angry then you should cut it off at that moment or recognition. Franklin's method was similarly based largely on a process of elimination. The major difference between Franklin's and Liao Fan's system is that while Franklin emphasized eliminating faults when noticed, Liao Fan's ledger placed additional emphasis on *going out of one's way to perform good deeds and service to others*, which is something I think you should teach children.

Liao Fan taught that, if you really want good fortune then it is necessary both to reform your thoughts and behavior and to practice kind deeds and selfless acts of merit that take care of others. Neither of these two aspects can be missing. He further explained that you must practice actively *three* types of giving to move ahead: the giving of wealth (by which you attain wealth in return), the giving of teachings (by which you gain intelligence and wisdom), and the giving of fearlessness, hope and confidence to others (by which you attain health and longevity).

Franklin was a go-getter who made efforts in many

fields of endeavors. Perhaps the reason he did not include more proactive steps (other than reforming errors) in his system was because he was naturally proactive in character. It was his natural character to start public initiatives in many fields, and so perhaps he didn't need to push himself to doing good deeds as much as Liao Fan had to do.

Regardless, my personal recommendation is that you combine Liao Fan's and Franklin's method to create your own daily journal of proactive efforts to create new merit other than just correcting and eliminating errors in your life. This is how to change your fate, fortune and destiny. Such a system will be instrumental in creating positive change in your life, and help you create the habit of energetic vigor that is needed to create a new future.

Chapter 4
FRANK BETTGER DISCOVERS THE
SECRET TO BUSINESS SUCCESS

Can Franklin's results be repeated? Can Liao Fan's lessons produce similar results in our life? Can these methods be applied to the field of business rather than just "self-improvement"?

The answer is yes to all of these questions.

Many have heard the story of Frank Bettger, who many years ago was a Major League Baseball infielder for the St. Louis Cardinals. An arm injury cut his career short, and he then ended up selling insurance for the Fidelity Mutual Life Insurance Company. He was initially a failure as an insurance salesman and was ready to quit, but turned his life around by changing his attitude.

As a resident of Philadelphia, he eventually became interested in Benjamin Franklin, one of its most famous sons, and began reading Franklin's autobiography (see chapter 3). Bettger realized that he could use its principles of self-improvement to both change himself and improve his sales skills.

Would it work? Bettger reasoned that Franklin was a

scientist and his plan was scientific. He recognized that while Franklin's method was not easy, no method is easy. However, applying its principles might be a definite way to better performance.

Should Bettger appropriate them to his own purposes and make the effort? Like Caesar, Bettger pondered the path ahead and then made the decision to cross the Rubicon. He said that he met many people who had heard of Franklin's original plan for moral improvement, but never met anyone who had applied it. He decided to use it.

Bettger later wrote of his efforts at doing this and their results in *How I Raised Myself from Failure to Success in Selling*, which has become a motivational classic.

Benjamin Franklin had dedicated more space in his autobiography to this method than anything else in the book, and said he owed much of his success and happiness in life to the self-improvement system he had created. Bettger became determined to apply its principles to the field of selling where he was not particularly successful and wanted to increase his income. He eventually found the method so successful that thereafter he felt every sales manager should make it mandatory that other salesmen follow a similar plan.

Bettger explained,

> I followed his plan exactly as he told me how he used it. I just took it and applied it to selling. Of Franklin's thirteen subjects, I chose six, then substituted seven others which I thought would be more helpful to me in my business, subjects in which I was especially weak.
>
> Here is my list, and the order in which I used them:
>
> 1. Enthusiasm.
> 2. Order: self-organization.
> 3. Think in terms of others' interests.

4. Questions.
5. Key issue.
6. Silence: listen.
7. Sincerity: deserve confidence.
8. Knowledge of my business.
9. Appreciation and praise.
10. Smile: happiness.
11. Remember names and faces
12. Service and prospecting.
13. Closing the sale: action.

I made up a 3" x 5" card, a "pocket reminder," for each one of my subjects, with a brief summary of the principles, … The first week, I carried the card on *Enthusiasm* in my pocket. At odd moments during the day, I read these principles. Just for that one week, I determined to double the amount of enthusiasm that I had been putting into my selling, and into my life. The second week, I carried my card on *Order: self-organization.* And so on each week.

After I completed the first thirteen weeks, and started all over again with my first subject—*Enthusiasm*—I knew I was getting a better hold on myself. I began to feel an inward power that I had never known before. Each week, I gained a clearer understanding of my subject. It got down deeper inside of me. My business became more interesting. It became exciting!

At the end of one year, I had completed four courses. I found myself doing things naturally, and unconsciously, that I wouldn't have attempted a year before. Although I fell far short of mastering any of these principles, I found this simple plan a truly magic formula. Without it, I doubt whether I could have maintained my enthusiasm … and I believe if a man can maintain enthusiasm long enough, it will produce anything![5]

Applying Franklin's method helped Frank Bettger improve his organizational and selling skills so much that Dale Carnegie once said that Bettger could have retired at age forty. A previous failure at insurance sales, by using this method Bettger become Top Salesman for twenty years at Fidelity Mutual. In fact, he went on to become one of the most successful insurance salesmen of his time.

In *How I Raised Myself from Failure to Success in Selling*, Bettger wrote that Franklin's method is one of the most practical ideas that he ever discovered in the field of selling and self-improvement. You can certainly use this method to improve your business and change your life, which I encourage.

Doubtless you can see how anyone can take the three systems - Liao Fan's, Franklin's and Bettger's adaptation - and create something similar that works for other fields such as sports. The idea of a systematic method of self-development can and should be able to help everyone. It may not look easy, but no method is easy. Nevertheless, it is a sure means for moving ahead.

---

[5] Frank Bettger, *How I Raised Myself From Failure to Success in Selling*, (New York: Simon & Schuster, 1981), pp. 187-188.

Chapter 5
DEVELOP NEW SKILLS THROUGH
DEEP DELIBERATE PRACTICE

What does it take to become great? The fields of business, athletics, science, mathematics, exploration, music, dance and the arts all have seen men and women of exceptional talent. Where did that talent come from? Where they just born with it, or did they develop it? What gets people to a stage of excellence that is far beyond the ordinary?

Deliberate Practice

Geoff Colvin, an editor at *Fortune* magazine, examined hundreds of research studies in order to find out, and then wrote *Talent is Overrated: What Really Separates World-Class Performers from Everybody Else.* His conclusion was that world-class performers do not succeed because of innate talent. Rather, individuals who practice in a special way, which is now called "deliberate practice," are the ones who become the leaders at the top levels of world-class talent and performance. Specifically, they engage in highly concentrated practice, which stretches them beyond their comfort zone, involving very particular activities they need to master to become great. They *practice deliberately* at improving specific behaviors that are the parts of a broader performance, and then link all those activities together into a total performance of excellence.

In other words, world-class talent can be learned, and the difference between ordinary performers and world-class/experts is usually a long period of deliberate practice devoted to improving performance in specific areas of need. People get very good at something because they work hard at it with deliberate practice, i.e. they develop their talent by working at what they cannot do in order to become better. To do so they employ specific goals and training measures, performance measurement and feedback systems and special types of mental practice.

Deliberate practice is a type of methodical training for incremental improvements to produce better final outcomes in any type of activity. It includes setting specific goals or objectives so that you know from the outset what you want, creating a training system, and it requires a monitoring or feedback procedure for identifying performance errors and providing insights that can be applied in further practice. When practicing to improve your skills, you don't just need to focus on a goal but need some way to see what isn't right so that you can correct any of your efforts. If you don't practice at something with a continuous feedback system then you won't get any better and will probably stop caring.

This sounds a lot like the previous systems we have been reviewing.

In other words, you don't need to be born with talent in order to learn how to excel. You just need to practice in a certain way and then at the minimum you will achieve above average performance. The more practice you do, of the deliberate type that stretches your skills, the higher the chances that you will become excellent or even outstanding.

Naturally in learning skills it helps if you have an exceptional coach, and of course the support of your family and a friendly environment, and employ certain types of mental training but the important point is that you can develop skill through a special type of deliberate practice. It takes work, but deliberate practice does work at developing skills, talents and expertise.

Even high-performing businesspeople, who seem to demonstrate exceptional skills of competence, usually practice those talents over and over again using essentially the same type of deliberate practice employed by athletes, musicians, artists and other talented individuals. Deliberate practice is an invitation to excellence and greatness, but it requires effort.

That effort is essentially no different, though perhaps more demanding, than the effort required to keep at Liao Fan's ledger of merits and demerits, Benjamin Franklin's ledger of virtuous improvement, or Frank Bettger's productivity system for sales success. It requires commitment to a disciplined process of training.

Achieving greatness, in terms of skills or ability, requires much sacrifice and dedication to a process. It requires a measure of continuous practice over time. Only time brings you significant life changes and greatness - just as only time brings you the greatest rewards of compound interest. Basically, the longer you systematically practice a skill to improve your proficiency, the better the compounding of results you will see over time. Long-term devotion to the cause of self-improvement (growing and developing a talent) is a significant undertaking, and you must recognize from the start that it will require many years to reach a point of real momentum. However, what separates the super skillful from others in the end is not the talent they begin with but the consistency of deliberate practice they employ to improve their skills, which requires a long term support system to keep it going.

Deep Practice

In Daniel Coyle's *The Talent Code: Greatness Isn't Born. It's Grown. Here's How*, the secrets of "deep practice" are also revealed. The talent greats of the world take a skill they wish to master, absorb the whole thing holistically, break it into component chunks or pieces, and then practice each piece to perfection before linking things back into one whole. After learning how to perform each piece perfectly, they progressively link larger and larger sections of perfect pieces together into a single whole.

To master a skill to a level of excellence you need to break it down into smaller component chunks and slowly perfect each piece through repetition (until you can repeat it seamlessly with perfection) before moving to the next. Doing this is "deep practice."

Some experts say that the level of deep practice required to master a skill is "10,000 practice hours," which references a theory developed by K. Anders Ericcson (author of *The Cambridge Handbook of Expertise and Expert Performance*). Of course the 10,000 hours is only indicative of the requirement for tremendous practice effort since it might only require a few thousand hours to master any particular talent.

The reason this works is because skill or talent is basically a memory and memory depends on neural pathways. The creation of memory is a biological process, and the creation of skill is dependent on mechanisms involving nerves and their wrappings called myelin.

The more you use a skill, the more solid your neural pathways for that skill become due to the increased traffic usage and the fact that more myelin wraps around that skill pathway in the brain. Thick myelin sheaths indicate a preferred pathway of neural usage, much like how a dirt road grows wider with greater and greater traffic.

Myelin can be built with constant practice, and so you want to deliberately and repeatedly build neural circuits that reflect optimum perfect performance. You don't want to build neural circuits for incorrect performances and then have to rewire the brain later to correct errors. You want to practice perfection from the start and allow as few errors as possible into the learning process.

You don't want to just develop perfect skills, but you want to practice excellence over and over again so that, as Coyle says, the neural pathways for optimal skills become sufficiently wrapped with myelin to the extent that they become the preferential circuits of usage.

Without a doubt, the anatomy of the brain does change as you build skills. For instance, studies of meditators not only show that meditation improves concentration and attention but that certain areas of the brain also become larger due to mindfulness practice. Most interestingly, a study of London taxi drivers discovered that the area in their brains governing spatial navigation was substantially larger than that of non-taxi drivers. It did not start out like that - it developed with time on the job.

Professional piano players also have more myelinated neural circuits (axons) in certain areas of the brain related to piano playing than ordinary people or ordinary piano players, and the amount of myelination is correlated with the amount of time they have spent practicing. It has been found that the amount of myelination around neural circuits definitely changes with the practice of a skill. In other words, your brain changes as you learn. As you learn a skill you develop new neural circuits in the brain, and as you repeatedly do things in a certain way you strengthen the corresponding network of neural paths in preference over others, which actually might be better or more optimal. This is why you want to learn perfection from the start.

The world famous neuro-scientist Richie Davidson has found that you can definitely train your brain to change, the change is measurable, and new ways of thinking can change it for the better. For instance, by focusing on wholesome thoughts, such as the virtues Franklin and Liao Fan desired, you can actually influence the plasticity of the brain and shape it in a way that can be beneficial. The virtues that Liao Fan and Benjamin Franklin strove to practice can actually be regarded as skills you can practice that will shape your brain (as well as your behavior) in wholesome, positive directions.

The implication of all this is that skill, and even greatness, is not innate. It is not born but is developed. You do not need to have a skill to start with in order to develop that talent. It is developed through effort; and the best type of effort for world-class skill is deliberate deep practice which requires that you commit yourself to a constant system of self-improvement. If you want to become an exceptional performer of any type, you need to practice a relevant form of deliberate effort.

Simply put, adults have a remarkable ability to learn and change through practice. You therefore do not need any innate skills in order to become great. People can become superior in some fashion if they simply train themselves more effectively. To excel you definitely have to work hard, but the key is to spend your practice time constructively using a form of well-designed deliberate practice that repeats excellence, so that it becomes ingrained, and gets you out of your comfort zone.

Sound familiar?

If talent and skill can be learned then there is no reason to complain that you are not talented. The correct way to think is that you are not talented *yet*. You haven't yet put in the required practice at the right type of exercises. If you want to learn a particular skill or develop a particular talent, then combine everything you have learned here into a schedule of deliberate deep practice.

Chapter 6
DEFY YOUR GENETIC PROGRAMMING

Most people think they are powerless to go against genetic propensities. They might gain weight much too easily because obesity runs in the family despite all sorts of diets, or worry about developing heart disease, Alzheimer's or diabetes because most of their relatives have it. With a fallen spirit, they often feel like there is nothing they can do about these things because, "It is all in my genes and runs in my family. I cannot go against my genetic destiny."

If you think genes control your life and you are the slave of genetic influences then you are mistaken. If you can change something as strong as fate, eliminate difficult character flaws, turn business failure into success and learn skills that are hard to master, why can't you live life in such a way as to put off, manage or even cure a type of illness that runs in your family?

Living life in a special disciplined sort of way, as we have been revealing, is sometimes all that is necessary to turn your health around or defy the genetic weaknesses that cause illness. Sometimes a profound change in your medical conditions can be accomplished by regular exercise and a permanent but simple change in the diet. Sometimes the only thing required to reverse a condition or stave it off is regularly taking the right vitamin/mineral supplements. Many things are possible, and they all involve the fact that your genes are not your destiny!

Don't overstate the role of genetics as a life influence. Don't ever believe that a certain illness or health condition in your life is fated due to your genes. We have seen that you are not the powerless victim of anything, but can rearrange your life to go against conditions to achieve outcomes previously thought impossible.

Basically, genes are not your destiny. Your health is controlled not just by your genes, but by other factors you can control such as your diet, lifestyle and environment. Those factors can override genetic influences, but in order for this to work you need to make positive changes in your life along those lines and stick to them with continual compliance.

Therefore, whether or not your genetic tendencies for illness are realized depends entirely upon how you live – what you eat, do and even think since thinking guides your actions. You just need to cultivate the proper knowledge and understanding (wisdom) in order to know what things to do to thwart the genetic tendencies that often produce unfavorable outcomes. Then you must *live life in such a way that those conditions never arise.*

Nutrition, for instance, definitely affects the way your genetic code is expressed. By changing your diet and by eating certain nutritional supplements you can reverse or delay (or manage) many diseases.

The presence of a strong social network, strong family bonds and regular religious practice helps people live longer. Why is it that these factors can override the genetic tendencies for shorter life spans? Since heart patients with a strong social support network also have a mortality rate $1/7^{th}$ of those who don't, why should we assume that it is our genes or even disease that controls our destinies?

When you use your mind in a more positive way it can affect your thoughts, moods and emotions all the way through to the curing of diseases and living longer. Your mind can definitely change your body. For instance, science has shown that the practice of meditation can affect the plasticity of your brain and its various neural connections. Meditation can reduce the gray matter in the amygdala, which is a region connected to anxiety and stress, and clinical studies show that regular meditation practice breaks the cycle of anxiety-creating thoughts. Meditation for thirty minutes a day can also boost your mood as much as antidepressants used for depression.

Studies have also shown that people who have been practicing meditation for more than five years are physiologically more than twelve years younger than their chronological age. Ainslie Meares in Australia found that image-free meditation even helped with cancer remissions. Meditators as a group also consistently have less than half the hospitalization of other groups with comparable ages, genders and professions.

Aren't all these results suggesting that your mental practice can help to override genetic predispositions?

Meditation is simply a lifestyle change and yet it can have all these measurable benefits *when practiced regularly.* Who, then, says genes are your destiny? The mind-body connection can definitely affect your health and well-being and sometimes help to overcome disease, and you can make use of that connection through the practice of meditation.

Speaking to the power of the mind, it has been found that people with a positive mental attitude (optimists) not only have stronger immune systems but have a 55% lower risk of death from all causes and 23% lower risk of fatal heart failure. They are less likely to catch a cold, recover from injuries quicker, and tend to live 7.5 years longer than other people.

All of these positive results are due to people using their minds differently, proving that our actions and behaviors, lifestyle changes and "soft factors" can indeed help to thwart the pull of genetic tendencies.

In terms of further science, years ago Dean Ornish astounded the medical community and transformed the way we think about health and well-being when he published *Dr. Dean Ornish's Program for Reversing Heart Disease.* The Ornish Plan showed that by making comprehensive changes in your lifestyle you could reverse even severe heart disease (sounds like Liao Fan, Franklin and Bettger). Many coronary heart disease benefits could even be attained after only one year's time - without the use of drugs!

Therefore, just because your parents or siblings have died from heart disease it doesn't mean that you will as well. You can do something about the risks to prevent this. Your might have a risk for heart disease as a genetic inheritance, but is not a destiny. To make sure it doesn't happen, however, like Caesar you must be willing to *fight.* You must go right against the causes of heart disease through diet, supplements, exercise, and meditation.

Heart disease is just an example we are using to show that you can intervene without medicine to positively thwart such a fate – just as you can go against the genetic predispositions for diabetes, cancer, obesity and many other conditions – and defy what you believe might be a death sentence. You just have to live smarter by making changes in your diet and lifestyle. You have to live differently than someone who has better genes for those conditions.

Isn't that just common sense rather than tossing your fate to genetics? And isn't by living your life differently how people normally distinguish themselves in the field of excellence and accomplishments?

Some conventional approaches to heart disease, such as intrusive practices like angioplasty and bypass surgery, are not just dangerous but often ineffective. They also cost billions of dollars per year in health systems across the world. However, a daily routine of living better with improved eating choices, fitting exercise, stress reduction techniques like meditation, and ample social support systems can actually prevent or reverse cardiovascular disease.

Doing so is simply a matter of setting up a system of changes, incorporating them into your life, and then staying with those changes. This is why people typically use checklists and schedules (like Liao Fan's, Franklin's and Bettger's) to help break old habits that are holding them back. The larger the health problems the larger the changes you will usually have to make in your life to eliminate them, and the larger the changes the more you will need a comprehensive system to help you make the necessary effort.

Let's say that you have a high genetic risk for heart disease. You now have the choice of having your chest cut open for surgery (such as angioplasty, a coronary bypass or stent insertion) or learning how to meditate, walk every day, stop smoking, eat better and even take some helpful vitamin/mineral supplements. Which road do you want to choose? I would rather roll the dice that my positive lifestyle changes will do the trick than roll the dice that doing nothing will win me a reprieve.

Research is showing that the more changes you make the better you usually get at reversing health conditions. As a general rule, if you want to alter a health condition you must start off by making a few changes and then make progressively larger changes until you achieve the goal you are after. As Franklin found, start small instead of trying to change everything all at the same time, and then work from there.

When you want to make changes in your fortune, character, business performance or level of skills, the roadblock involves continually arousing the effort to work at creating a new lifestyle over the long-run. This is the problem of keeping up your initial motivation that medicine calls the challenge of compliance.

Ornish and his colleagues recently published another surprising study confirming everything we have already been discussing. This scientific study found that better nutrition, stress management techniques, walking and psychosocial support actually changed the expression of over 500 genes in men with early-stage prostate cancer. For men with early prostate cancer, his published program could favorably express or change genes and stop or even reverse the disease.

In other words, while scientists don't quite understand the mechanisms as to why, studies show that lifestyle changes may slow, stop or even reverse the progression of prostate cancer. Thus, they can override a problem intertwined with our genetics. Doubtless this route can affect many other diseases as well.

Positive lifestyle interventions (without medications) have indeed been shown to lower blood pressure, improve cholesterol levels, increase the length of telomeres (the ends of chromosomes that control aging), reduce the frequency of cardiac events for those with heart disease, and counter a host of other health conditions.

So changing what you eat and how you live can positively alter how your genes are expressed. If there is a tendency in your family you want to avoid, then live life in the ways that would manage it in order to prevent it. Arrange your diet, nutritional supplements, exercise routines and lifestyle to determine your heath rather than let genes control your destiny.

For instance, there are thousands of fruit and vegetable substances you can add to your diet that are good for your health, improve medical conditions and proactively protect against disease. This is why I recommend people consume nutrient-dense superfood green or red powders on a daily basis. In easily digestible and assimilable form they contain the concentrated phytochemicals of dozens of fruits, vegetables, herbs, vitamins and minerals that would not normally be available to the diet and yet can be used to repair DNA.

The Family Tree

Here is an effective little process I use to help guide people towards positive lifestyle changes and natural interventions that can change their life and help stave off genetic predispositions.

First, create a family tree of all your natural family members including brothers and sisters, parents and grandparents and all your aunts and uncles. Extend your family tree to make it as large and as comprehensive as possible.

Now, underneath each person's name write down any major health conditions they suffer from or have suffered in the past as well as the cause of death if an individual has passed away. These items might include health conditions such as diabetes, osteoporosis, high blood pressure, low blood pressure, allergies, arthritis, Alzheimer's, depression, heart disease and causes of death such as cancer, stroke, or renal failure. Write down whatever you can remember.

Next, circle any related conditions that seem to be repeated across the family members, which is a simple but quick way of getting a handle on your unhealthy genetic potentials.

Now comes the difficult part. Look at the common conditions you have found and start reading books or internet articles about the natural lifestyle changes, dietary changes and supplements used to cure, manage, mitigate or avoid them (such as at www.lef.org). These are what you should consider adopting whenever a health condition arises.

For instance, say you suffered from constipation and heart disease runs in your family. Magnesium is one of the supplements commonly used to help both heart disease and constipation, so of all the possible assists you might consider magnesium would certainly be among your top choices, especially if blood tests then also revealed that you had low magnesium levels.

To make positive life changes you have to think outside the box like this because the orthodox way doesn't always consider these things. With a nutritionist, naturopath or complementary physician's help you might thereby be able to avoid the inevitable prescription drugs or surgeries for a pre-existing health condition. You might even be able to reverse your conditions. How? By making changes that cure you and thus render drugs or surgery unnecessary. Unfortunately, big medicine and big money will cooperatively try to dissuade you from trying these possibilities.

For instance, despite tens of thousands of scientific studies there are members of the mass media, health care professionals, and others who appear to have the agenda that vitamin/mineral supplements are a complete waste of money no matter their cost. They commonly promote the idea that as long as you eat a "healthy" diet then supplements have no value to anyone no matter what their health status. They often push aside the facts that supplements and lifestyle changes can reduce medical symptoms and improve the quality of life for chronically ill patients.

This type of behavior is unethical, and these views are just nonsense and shoddy thinking.

Fish-eaters, for instance, have fewer heart attacks and fewer cases of sudden death caused by an irregular heartbeat. That being the case, why not tell heart patients to add fish to their diet or high-quality fish oil capsules as an alternative? It is true that lifestyle or supplemental interventions don't lead to uniform positive outcomes 100% of the time, *but what does in life?* That's hardly an argument against them.

You must use your brain and start thinking for yourself if you want to forge new positive life outcomes. Caesar would certainly toss aside nonsensical thinking and eat certain foods (or supplements) if they helped him feel better or made him more effective. He wouldn't wait for some scientific study to tell him what to try, and would guide himself by his own practical experience.

You have to take charge of your life and assume responsibility for your fate if you want to change it. If we assume that we are just the victim of bad genes, bad karma, bad fate or bad luck then there is not much we can do about it other than just to suffer our destiny. However, to the degree that we take proactive steps and do something about conditions we are free to fashion new outcomes and positively change our fortune. Unfortunately, you will have to rally the courage and energy to go against common thinking if you want to do this.

Genetics do play a role in your health and well-being, but more for some and less for others. There are differences in outcomes even for twins in the same family. The truth is our health and well being is not decided by fate, it is decided by ourselves through the actions (and non-actions) we take.

Therefore, don't lay down your command and give your fate over to someone else. Move forward by choosing to take charge over your genetic destiny.

Chapter 7
ATTAIN SPIRITUAL PROGRESS WHERE NONE WAS THOUGHT POSSIBLE

In the east you commonly hear of sages and saints who have attained spiritual enlightenment, which is considered the apex of spiritual achievements. Many know that achieving enlightenment is a difficult task yet few know what this really means or entails. A simple explanation is as follows.

As human beings we often ask ourselves where our lives, where the world, and where consciousness and the universe all come from. The whole universe must come from something prior, but what is It? What is the most prior or original substance of the universe and all Creation? What is that absolute most nature?

Whatever It is, we can call It the original nature, fundamental essence, absolute essence or primal state. It takes on different names in religion like Parabrahman, Wuji, Shiva, Father, Allah, Ayin, Ein Sof, absolute reality, True Self, True Reality, dharmakaya, nirvana, Nameless One, First Principle, Self, fundamental essence, original nature, self-nature or Buddha nature. Self-existent and self-manifest (not born from something else), eternal, blissful, motionless and pure, It is unlike everything else that comes from It because all subsequent emanates have attributes and being the purest It has none. Everything must be within It and come from It so as to be fully permeated by It to the last, but It must be different from all of the substances, phenomena or evolutes that originate from It in a very special way as I will explain.

Emanation

The ultimate original essence or substance of the universe must be one thing (substance or essence). It must be perfectly pure, homogenously whole, indivisible, undifferentiated, attributeless, infinite, all-pervasive, unmoving, unchangeable, eternal and actionless. As the *absolute* essence, it must be homogenous and perfectly pure. There cannot be anything other than it that is more primordial, and so It must be the original state, original essence or original nature of everything. Because of perfect purity It cannot move, change or become altered but must always remain the original substance that It is. Because it never changes it has no precedent stage nor consequent stage and thus is birthless, deathless, and eternal.

Because It is unmoving and unchangeable, nothing can ever happen to It and It cannot cause anything, thus by nature it must be actionless. However, somehow this original nature that is motionless because of homogenous purity inexplicably gives rise to an emanation (different from It and yet of It) that eventually, through countless subsequent transformations, produces us and the world we see.

There must be a first emanation from this pure and unmoving primal essence, and the only thing we can say about how that movement and manifestation arises out of a changeless essence is that no one knows or can explain how it can happen. That is what "ignorance" is, namely we don't know how it happens and yet it does. No one can conceive of a cause for "emanation" and so It – the purest and highest - is the causeless cause of all existence even though it cannot cause anything else because it does not change or move; being changeless it can never change or cause change.

The school of Vedanta explains that True Reality – the absolute original nature that never moves or changes - somehow gives rise to various realms of attributes and movement. Since that original nature is prior most to everything, and never moves or changes, It is the only real and dependable thing in the universe, and hence It is our real Self, True Self, our ultimate nature. It is our fundamental self-nature.

The first emanate from It somehow appears just as a puff of wind manifests in the sky without us being able to trace its origins. That puff of wind is different from the space in which it appears, yet it doesn't distort the sky in any way. There isn't any distortion in the sky if light passes through it either, is there? Space is not affected by the light or wind that passes through it.

Therefore, since wind can flow in the sky without distorting it in any way, similarly all the substances with attributes which originate (as eventual emanations) from the primal essence can arise within that pure original nature without causing any perturbations or changes to It at all. It is like space (without attributes) and they are like phenomena that arise within space without perturbing it in any way. Furthermore, just as the wind and the motionless sky are not visible entities but there is a great deal of difference between the two, so there is a difference between the primal original essence and all subsequent evolutes even though they reside within It, are essentially composed of It and are permeated by It. Despite their different forms, It still remains as their fundamental essence, their true self-nature, their original source.

The original nature never changes, but emanation from

It somehow appears (without us knowing how) and kicks off a continuous process of transformation which, through the continuity of cause and effect, continues in time giving birth to more and more emanations that we can consider further condensations, solidifications, evolutions or transformations of the original substance. How long has this process continued? Is it simply billions of years old as astronomers speculate, or does the age entail uncountable eons? Or, does it entail beginninglessness, meaning that the original nature and manifest emanations (phenomena) have always co-existed?

Eastern religions don't postulate a Big Bang or finite Creation point but rather a beginningless and never ending process of unfolding, emanation, evolution and transformation. The process of emanation is considered beginningless, meaning it has always been so and has never first appeared. There is no beginning to it (so it is uncaused) and there will be no end to it. No one can determine that Creation (transformation) starts from something or that it will become something definite since it is always changing with ceaseless motion.

Sequentially More Subtle Stages of Matter

Now let's take this all from an opposite angle so it is easier to understand. If you have in your hand an ice cube you know that it is solid. Now ask yourself what is the next higher energy state than the solid ice cube? What is a *more subtle* state of matter? Water, because if the ice cube melts you get liquid.

Now, what is the next higher energy state of water rather than being liquid? The answer is steam, which appears when you add more energy to water. You can consider steam as a more *subtle state* of matter that is akin to gas or the air element. In this type of thinking, gas is far "more subtle" than liquid.

What is more subtle than gas? You might say energy

since it is absent of all coarse matter, but we'll skip that stage and proceed to space, the element within which energy and gas appears.

Why space? Space is empty of everything and thus is more refined, "more subtle" or "more pure" than gas or energy (which is free of coarse matter). It is clear (empty or void), vast and nonmoving, yet because it has properties it still is an element whereas no such properties exist in the original nature at all.

Naturally this is just a way of talking so that you can get the idea of a sequence of "higher essences," which can be understood as *more refined, subtle or purer* states of existence. Think of them as "higher" or *more subtle* substances or phases that transcend lower substances, energies or planes of existence. You can arrive at them through the transformation of the lower substances.

What is more subtle than space? This is a tricky one, because the answer is consciousness. How can that be? Why is it consciousness? You can arrive at this answer from the following.

Everything you see in the world appears within your mind, correct? You see this book, television, the sky, people; everything is appearing within your consciousness. Even the space you now see in your mind that exists between your eyes and the wall of your room appears in your consciousness as an image, right? That image of space is something empty and pure, but you see space within your consciousness while *you do not see consciousness itself.* Consciousness is therefore more subtle than space! You can see space but you cannot see the substance of consciousness.

Consciousness is therefore even more subtle (refined) than space and you can't see it. You just see space, but not the substance of consciousness from which space is formed in your mind. You have just proved that consciousness is more subtle than space.

The energy or substance of consciousness itself is in

some way a subtle substance in which space appears but is more subtle or refined than space, which is why no one is aware of it. Consciousness cannot form an image of itself so you cannot "see" consciousness because pure consciousness cannot form an image of what it is; any image of it is other than what it is because the image would be of a "thing" rather than consciousness essence, and so if consciousness were to "see" itself the net result would be nothingness or emptiness; consciousness experiencing itself is just consciousness and so there is no change or recognition of anything at all.

Only someone who attains enlightenment can realize the foundational substance of consciousness – a substance or Supra-Causal stage of energy that is ultimate substratum of thoughts in the mind and also the Mother of matter. They can do this because they eventually develop (cultivate) a spiritual body composed of that very same Supra-Causal substance, which is the same substance that composes the material universe as its purest substrate energy essence.

Just as we are within space and space also permeates us, space and the environment of matter around us are all residing within a higher energy matrix (substance) that is their foundational substance transcending them. It is a refined substance, material phase or subtle energy that is always naturally there in the environment and yet we don't experience its pure essence because it is too high, pure, subtle, transcendental or refined. Only if you possess a spiritual body composed of that substance can you then know what it is for otherwise you cannot reach it to know about it (except through logic and inference).

To realize enlightenment is equivalent to having generated a spiritual body of that very refined substance and therefore being able to realize its essence. Hence, to realize enlightenment is equivalent to discovering (becoming familiar with) the root essence (fundamental substance) of matter and consciousness which are both ultimately composed of that "very refined substance" (which Xuan Zang called the "purest, clearest, highest") and that Supra-Causal substance in turn is composed of higher, more refined essences, too.

In its resting state the substance of consciousness doesn't move, and since a mind without thoughts seems that it is just empty, for this reason spiritual schools use the analogy of cultivating an empty or formless mind as a way of propelling you forward to cultivating that particular spiritual body. They also speak of cultivating "clear awareness" or "pristine awareness" which carries exactly the same connotations as pure consciousness without expression as a thought (movement, mark, sign or attribute) and point you in the right direction. You never try to destroy thoughts or forbid them in this cultivation process but simply use different practice exercises to purify the various energy bases of your body and mind. The effort to do so takes much work.

We must train through spiritual exercises to be able to get to this higher level of being so that we are able to experience the purest levels of the mind and matter. Since consciousness is ultimately due to this Supra-Causal energy, the precursor of consciousness is this "very refined substance" alternatively known as the "purest, clearest, highest" or "clear light." In other words, attaining enlightenment means reaching the state of the highest, purest and clearest (energy-matter-substance-essence) that is also the foundational substance of matter and energy. It is just above their level of "density," and thus is the creation level energy or substance just above (transcending) the vital energy of consciousness and spiritual beingness.

The path of mental training to reach this stage of attainment/development eventually entails cultivating a realm of infinite pure awareness that remains open, free and alive whether or not there are any modifications (thoughts) within it. You *don't try to block thoughts* to experience "nothingness or no-thought" but cultivate a detachment of thoughts so that they die down and your mental realm stays alive while its background becomes one of empty clarity. Buddhism calls this consciousness without a mark, attribute or sign, meaning expression (thought). Hence, meditation is and should be the basic spiritual pathway for all religions.

As a human being, the way to arrive at an experience similar to the nature of this substance is through the practice of meditation that abandons mental disturbances until they all die down and your mind becomes clear. When pure awareness is left, without any forced mental modifications (thoughts), and it shines freely without being forcefully obstructed to block thoughts from arising, then this is called cultivating spiritual illumination, pristine awareness or the clear light of the mind. It is similar to experiencing the root energy of consciousness in its purest form, which is why meditation is the primary road of spiritual practice used to take people to enlightenment.

The Root Substance of Consciousness and Matter

Sages of sufficient achievement always explain that consciousness and matter are both made of a fundamental Supra-Causal energy, but they call it by different names. In India they call it original *prana,* primordial *prana* or heavenly *prana* while in China the equivalent to "*prana*" is "Qi" and this foundational substance is called "Later Heavenly Qi." In Tibet it is referred to using terms like "clear light" although it is not a light composed of photons or anything else material at all; it is a precursor to the energies an particles or states we know of through science. In Christianity it is "uncreated light" or universal illumination.

Heavenly *prana* is not the primal first emanation, but it is an emanation just above the entire lower realm of matter and energy we call the realm of the five elements, so it is their "root source" precursor but not their primal root source. You don't even have to think of it as an "emanation" from the original nature but as simply the next higher, more refined stage of matter that is the subsequently higher substrate substance. It is not the True Self or absolute primordial essence. Nonetheless, to reach enlightenment means to become able to access this transcending realm while there are other realms higher still (more subtle).

Someone who becomes enlightened is an individual who realizes this higher Supra-Causal energy level of heavenly *prana*, which is the root source of the mind in terms of energy, and thus is called a sage or master. Through spiritual cultivation exercises they attain a spiritual body composed of this Supra-Causal level of *prana*, or Later Heavenly Qi and thereby develop various miraculous powers to use as they like.

Their body and consciousness-substance are composed of this energy, which spans the cosmic level created out of it, and so their level of awareness can extend to the "lower realms" that have it as their substrate. Hence their awareness can be said to be infinite, vast, cosmic or universal according to their degree of cultivation since the substance of their body-mind complex is composed of the transcending substratum beneath material creation and consciousness, meaning the consciousness of all sentient beings. This is why we hear terms from sages such as "universal illumination," "cosmic consciousness," "infinite mind." Actually your mind is limited, but is of this more refined substance and thus can know more things if you concentrate on the lower energy forms. How "infinite" your mind is depends on how much training you do learning how to recognize any vibrations that arise within the denser levels of manifestation. For instance, with training as a child you learn to recognize what is a book, apple, car and so forth; with a higher body you must also learn how to recognize all the inputs you can access with your mind/consciousness that is composed of a more refined substance/energy that permeates the environment everywhere. Consciousness is made of an energy; it isn't a nothingness. The consciousness of an enlightened being is now made of an energy or material that is a higher substratum than all previous lower bodies and therefore has access to more inputs that the lower body has.

In other words, just as you know all the thoughts within your mind, a person who develops a higher spiritual body composed of this transcending substance can also know all the things which arise within their own mind, too. It's just a body double at a higher energy level. At a sufficient level they can know/sense all the vibrations of the universe made of lower energies since those vibrations will be accessible to their consciousness if they like. With a body-mind composed of the universal Qi, given sufficient training they can learn to recognize specific vibrations that arise within the lower realms, such as mantra sounds or the specific thoughts of sentient beings - particularly when a human thinks of them - and can then act to address any calls for help from lower beings through their higher energy bodies.

The way to cultivate towards this achievement starts by using meditation to cultivate a clear mind of awareness (illumination), called emptiness or empty mind. Cultivating meditation is the road for attaining all the higher spiritual states of being, and it is the one reliable practice that starts the process of forming higher subtle bodies that can access the higher, more subtle realms. If you can develop through meditation a clear mind that does not become scattered or lost in thought, then you are on the correct spiritual path. You will begin to be able to develop spiritual progress where you thought none was possible.

To review, enlightenment is simply the act of reaching the root substance-energy level of our life force and mind (consciousness) which happens to transcend all the subsequent emanation levels of energy and matter beneath it, and thus it perfectly pervades the universe within it. This Supra-Causal level of substance/energy can be experienced only when you attain a higher spiritual body of that Later Heavenly Qi (universal Creation Qi) which permeates everywhere. The road of development involves your consciousness becoming purified of defiling mental states, which is why you practice meditation and other spiritual exercises.

On the road of spiritual practice you want to develop clear awareness where your mind seems quiet but is crisp, sharp and clear so that it can know-recognize all its own thoughts completely. At a much higher stage you eventually cultivate as a target a temporary state where consciousness exists singly and solely as shining all by itself without a subject-doer or object. At that time the experience is of "nothingness" since there are no thoughts. Even so, when you reach that experience of the pure substance of consciousness itself without perturbations (actually this is just a way of speaking because the substance/energy is moving rapidly but you just don't have the thoughts to cognize-cogitate anything) you afterwards must realize that it is not yet the experience of the highest nature. The Supra-Causal substance that is the root of consciousness, called heavenly Qi or heavenly *prana*, is still a lower level evolutionary "emanation," "condensation," "solidification" or "transformation" of yet higher essences, and so when you experience it in its purity you have not reached the highest level of enlightenment.

Now *prana* is very subtle and the ordinary mind cannot see it, but it is moving at an extremely rapid pace. Like a stream that seems motionless on the surface whereas the water is flowing tremendously fast, *prana* is always moving very quickly and ceaselessly transforming. That is why thoughts always arise in the mind through ceaseless transformations. At the root, it is because the substrate is always moving. As the Mother substrate beneath all consciousness (as well as matter) in the universe, *prana's* constant movement is the reason you will always have thoughts that change and transform from one thing into the next in manifold ways.

To become enlightened, you have to cultivate to a state where you can realize *prana,* where you develop an independent living body made of this *prana.* You cannot see it because it is the energy substrate from which your life force and consciousness are derived, so you have to cultivate a body to that level to experience it directly. This, of course, is still not the highest spiritual state you can reach, but through this attainment you realize and can *master* the root source of all subsequent creation realms, phases, energies or substances below it, so enlightenment is therefore called realizing the Creator or becoming one with the Creator. The "Creator" at the stage of enlightenment is not the ultimate source of Creation, but just an interim stage in the entire process of manifestation – the Supra-Causal energy stage of *prana* or Later Heavenly Qi.

The Two Aspects of *Prana*

Like the elements of solid, liquid, gas and so forth that exist within empty space, this Supra-Causal *prana* itself exists in/as a higher (purer, emptier, more refined or more subtle) substance (Early Heavenly Qi) and itself can be partitioned into two phases that seem like different entities but which are not. The substance of *prana* has two aspects: (1) there is the active stage of *prana* that refers to when it is moving (and thus manifesting as something – marks, phenomena, attributes, characteristics, signs, etc.), and (2) an unmoving state of *prana* that represents the "potential" or *unmanifest* side of material Creation, which *in terms of cultivation practice* simply means a state where thoughts are not born.

This unmanifest aspect of Heavenly *prana* or Supra-Causal energy is described using the analogy of an absolute vacuum of nothingness (or empty space) that has the potential for change and is considered a higher, purer, emptier, more refined or more subtle state than active *prana* since within it there seem to be no movements, vibrations or modifications. There seem to be no such things because to know this stage you must abandon thoughts. Actually *prana* is always moving very fast so it has no stage of motionless rest, and this "higher state" just refers to a stage wherein there are no thoughts to know it or anything - a samadhi of ignorance. We simply call it a motionless stage for expediency sake to help cultivators reach this stage temporarily since cultivating it briefly is necessary for attaining a yet higher body.

The unmanifest aspect or state of "nothingness" (a term for what it is like to experience unmoving *prana* or unmoving consciousness) is still the same Supra-Causal *prana* energy but this more subtle, undisturbed state of non-movement seems non-existent to lower forces, including the stage of active *prana*, and so is often referred to as "nothingness." This description of nothingness (freedom from thought) as a stage of Creation helps inspire spiritual practitioners to cultivate freedom from thought attachments so that thoughts die down and they can truly experience an empty mind. You cannot reach the experience by blocking or suppressing thoughts or by binding them up, but only by letting go of them so that they perfectly die down and clear stillness naturally (not forcefully) results. You should always allow thoughts to be born but just refrain from attaching to them. That is why the path of meditation never blocks thoughts to get to a state of "no-thought."

These two aspects, the unmanifest and manifest or potential and active, are often called the "yin" and "yang" aspects of manifestation. By specifying that there are two opposite states this helps cultivators know that they must cultivate (1) a quiet state of mind as opposed to (2) a more active mental state (whereas the quiet state is also active but at a level you cannot yet know).

Some spiritual schools say that the yin aspect appears before the yang aspect in the universal sequence of manifestation, meaning that "nothingness" (motionless *prana*) appears as an evolute before a movement, throbbing or pulsation appears within it (moving *prana*). In other words, the stage of Supra-Causal *prana* as a pure unmoving essence appears before the inspiration of movement initiates within it, after which it mistakenly seems as if there are two separate substances. Some schools say that these two sides appeared simultaneously, and some schools simply say that a higher essence splits into these two aspects of yin and yang without specifying any precedence.

Actually, *prana* is always moving, and the stage of "potential," "unmanifest," "unborn" or motionlessness simply means that thoughts have not yet been born though the substance of *prana* is always actively moving at a tremendously rapid pace. It is always moving at an extremely high frequency that makes it super ethereal (refined or intangible) and thus extremely powerful since energy level is related to frequency. Therefore the way to describe it correctly on a cosmic level is that Supra-Causal *prana* as an essence is there before (living beings and) consciousness evolutionarily develops within it so that thoughts can be born, but those at lower levels can through hard work cultivate a sequence of spiritual bodies and eventually one composed of that substance. For expedience sake and as a form of skillful means in teaching to lead people upwards in meditation progress, we avoid this whole explanation and just say that the pure stage of *prana* is unmoving, which can never really occur in reality.

For our purposes it really doesn't matter, but scholars like to argue about these things. Only sages with the highest stages of spiritual attainment could say for sure. The best way to think of it, however, is that when the vibrations of consciousness (thoughts) die down and totally disappear – which therefore negates the I-center of the mind created by thoughts (around which all other thoughts revolve) - then the experience of the world will disappear because the perturbations of consciousness will disappear; the knower will be non-existent. This is a temporary spiritual experience.

Describing the experience, some Hindu spiritual schools say that the energy that comprises consciousness will rest in only its pure self without any perturbations, modifications or disturbances (that are thoughts). Actually, there will still be movements, perturbations and modifications of the body-mind energy matrix but just no thoughts of recognition, which is a state of ignorance or nothingness. We simply colloquially call this the pure essence of *prana* in its unmanifest form, with "unmanifest" meaning the lack of thoughts or an I-center (namely consciousness) to know it rather than that *prana* isn't really a tangible substance and doesn't really have a form.

Sages from many religions say you can cultivate an experience of nothingness where the world disappears (*everything* disappears). Without an I-center due to moving *prana* at that time, there are no thoughts so *prana* is just experiencing itself (which is basically not any experience at all, and hence nothingness). This is also called a state of *pure being* or *pure existence* that sages cultivate as a training practice, but never as a permanent state. It is not considered enlightenment, nirvana, moksha, liberation or salvation because there is no knowledge of the world in this state, and so it is sometimes called a "samadhi of ignorance." It is worthless as a realm of experience, but there are some benefits to achieving this capability as a station of practice.

If you can reach this spiritual state you are experiencing just what you ultimately are that "isn't a person," but not yet your primordial most original substance that is ultimately what you are. This stage of Supra-Causal *prana* is not your fundamental substance, true self-nature or True

Self that the whole universe has evolved from. The experience of nothingness is a high spiritual experience, but not yet the experience of your *absolute* original nature or True Self. It is just an experience of the Supra-Causal energy level ultimately responsible for all matter and consciousness in the universe, but not the ultimate root source of consciousness and everything else.

Most people take their mental process as being themselves (their true spiritual self) but what they really are (because of what they come from) is a conditional agglomeration of higher essences in various forms and stages of emanation that originate from this Supra-Causal energy. Since all things are composed of these substances that intertwine in infinite causality nets of cross-definition, no being is an independent self. That conditional agglomeration has, because of endless chains of cause and effect, eventually evolved into a person over ageless time while other agglomerations have evolved into other things. Some of that essence has evolved into atoms and chemicals, some has become forces of nature such as magnetism or gravity, some has become unconscious life such as plants, and some has become animals such as yourself that have the capacity of thought. Thoughts have simply allowed us, and other beings in the universe, to discover a way within the universe to cultivate to realize our ultimate source state. There is really no such thing as sentience or sentient beings. Rather, there are just biological mechanisms (made of all these substances) that have evolved the power to form memories and thoughts. Thoughts, the ability to know things, are what consciousness is. This is what separates us from the other types of creations in existence.

When you say "I," what you really are referring to is your absolute original nature (the most fundamental substance of the cosmos), which means that all "I's" are fundamentally equal since they all point to he same thing – the common shared root. However, "I" could colloquially refer to the core substance of Supra-Causal heavenly *prana* that composes the material universe, too. In truth, however, everyone who says "I" is referring to the same one original substance (some call it "God") since we are all cause and effect transformations of its essence. Since everything is composed of this substance, everything is ultimately One is one wholeness or oneness that contains diversity linked in unity.

Because your mind disappears during the experience of nothingness – that we call *pure prana* without perturbations whereas it is actually a state of moving *prana* without mental recognitions - then the I-sense disappears. The mind only exists because there is the sense of being an individual I; the mind *is* the sense of being a personal I due to the existence of thoughts. Your "I" is not a permanent self-existent thing and there is no such thing as an actual independently existing I-self (independently existing apart from everything else) since you really are the fundamental essence that has become a certain shape and form, and which exists because of the interpenetration of countless cause and effect chains and forces. Nonetheless, at the stage of enlightenment you realize this foundational Supra-Causal "clear light" substance that produces/underlies the mind (because one attains a body composed of that material), and the corresponding mental experience is a perfectly clear, formless consciousness that is profoundly quiet when there are no thoughts. On a true spiritual path you don't suppress thoughts to "know/realize emptiness" but try to cultivate a crystal clarity of mind (pristine awareness) that knows all the thoughts of your mind, even the most subtle or hidden. This is always what you should try to cultivate as true spiritual practice.

We call this "spiritual illumination," which simply means a great clarity of mind. Even when there are no thoughts the mind is always alive and aware, ready for thoughts to arise and be known. When we talk about awareness shining behind our thoughts and emotions this refers to this same stage of achievement, i.e. it refers to that same material substance ("clear light") that is pure and unmoving of which thoughts (and bodies) are ultimately composed at their deepest substratum, but which seems non-existent (empty) when they are not there.

The idea of experiencing just pure awareness, pure consciousness or pure witnessing where there are no thoughts - and so the "knowing" actually means *not* knowing anything (you can similarly say that consciousness "only knows itself" or the substance of consciousness just rests in itself without any modifications) - means an experience of *nothingness* (no experiential realm) since without mental modifications there can be no subject to know an object and no object as a potential experience for a subject. You might say, "both ends (subject and object) are empty" to denote this. Nothingness or the non-appearance of the world is valueless in life, so you don't want to cultivate that. You want to cultivate a state where the mind has full clear knowing when there are thoughts, and is empty/quiet/more peaceful when there are no thoughts but always ready to give rise to thoughts. You want to be able to know all the subtle thoughts of your mind.

The important point to realize is that you can cultivate this capability through meditation, and thus meditation (such as vipassana) is true spiritual practice. At the very highest stages you can attain an experience of nothingness, which is a more subtle experience than the manifestation of thoughts within consciousness, but this is hard to attain, only temporary, of little use for existence and surpassed when you attain a yet higher (more subtle) body attainment.

In summary, when consciousness is freed of all vibrations, disturbances, movements, emanations or thoughts – however you wish to word it – the experience of nothingness results. It is like an absolute vacuum wherein there is nothing at all, and thus the experience is termed "emptiness," "nothingness," or "Unmanifest Causal." Within that unmanifest state of consciousness-substance eventually appears the arising of active (moving) *prana* and then all other subsequent evolutes. The ordinary mind is based on the *prana* of these two states which exist as its ultimate substratum layer, and that's why you cultivate meditation on the spiritual path.

So Manifest Supra-Causal universal active energy is eventually generated from the Unmanifest Supra-Causal aspect of the universe, meaning that forms take shape out of an infinite undefined chaotic energy matrix. Eventually gross manifestations appear as subsequent transformations of this stage of Supra-Causal universal *prana* energy (Later Heavenly Qi). This energy comes from a state that seems like a vacuum (just as matter appears in empty space), but is itself inside of higher and higher levels of energy (such as Early Heavenly Qi). When inactive, we say it has the potential to transform into anything just as a mind free of thought can give rise to various thoughts.

Let's go one stage higher. Denser substances are always composed of higher frequency, more refined, more subtle or more ethereal energies-substances-essences. The substance immediately above the *prana* or clear light stage is Early Heavenly Qi, but that still isn't the fundamental original nature. However, it is indeed an essence or substance that is different from the two yin and yang natures of Later Heavenly Qi, namely (2) the pure, formless or "more resting" substance of *prana* (Unmanifest Supra-Causal) that lacks definite forms and (2) active, vibrational or form-stage *prana*. Hence it is above the yin and yang natures of material creation, and thus above our body-mind complex.

To classify it, we shouldn't say it is the chaotic or "formless" stage of nothingness (emptiness). It is not any "form" or manifestation-activation stage of *prana* either. Hence, it is "neither the form nor formlessness" stages of emanation. To denote that it is different from *prana* it is said to be "neither with attributes or without attributes." Buddhism says it is "neither thought nor no-thought" to negate both the yin and yang states of *prana.*

These negative descriptions are just a way of giving it a name to denote that it – Early Heavenly Qi - is higher than the immediately lower substrate of Later Heavenly Qi (and its two stages) it eventually produces; it is higher than the yin and yang natures of heavenly *prana.* It is an essence we denote by negating both phases of its subsequently lower/denser nature, saying it is neither formless nor form (the two yin and yang subsequent levels); neither with attributes or without attributes, neither nothingness (the experience where consciousness is pure by itself) nor active consciousness (the realm of vibrating *prana* in manifestation); neither manifest consciousness nor unmanifest consciousness (which simply resides as a pure potential), and neither thought nor no-thought (thoughtlessness).

Those are some of ways used to denote the substance (Early Heavenly Qi) just transcending the foundational substance of consciousness, which is described as a clear light since that means it is so refined that it appears empty, intangible and invisible to the mind and yet provides awareness (like light). They help us describe its ultra-subtle nature that, like the original nature Itself, omnipresently permeates every transformational stage (emanate) beneath it completely.

If someone realizes the clear light stage of *prana* or Later Heavenly Qi which we also call "emptiness," this is considered initial enlightenment because they realize the subtle nature of the substance that is the bedrock of consciousness. This is why sages are able to know other people's thoughts naturally; they do so using a body-mind composed of this element and hence can know the thoughts of others since those thoughts have a foundation of this highest, most subtle substance as their substratum. If someone decides to work towards realizing the primordial original nature or ultimate One source of all that transcends everything – True Self, Buddha nature, Parabrahman, absolute reality, fundamental essence - they must attain a body composed of a substance higher than the substance of consciousness (clear light, Later Heavenly Qi or heavenly *prana*) that itself can be functioning within us as "manifest or unmanifest consciousness." Then, through the purity of that body vehicle and accompanying pure mind they will become able to realize its own motionless state of purity - what we provisionally term the original nature. To do this is considered full enlightenment and is called "becoming a Buddha."

You probably have never heard of this explanation, but many spiritual texts (the Jewish Kabbalah, Buddhist *Diamond Sutra, I-Ching* of Chinese culture, *Dasbodh* of Sri Samarth Ramdas and talks of *Sri Siddharameshwar Maharaj,* etc.) refer to these same stages of emanation, materialization, condensation, densification, crystallization, evolution or transformation. Each stage of emanation can be divided into a yin and yang aspect, or (relatively) motionless and active aspect, and the root aspect of the first emanation follows this same pattern with the True Self (Shiva, Buddha nature, absolute nature, etc.) being the absolute yin nature of the universe that never move, never gives birth, never changes and thus always stay eternal and constant. Shakti, or the Grand Illusory Play, is considered the active (yang) opposite of the absolute self-nature which somehow appears within It and is always dancing, always changing, always moving, always transforming. Everything is a transformation of Shakti within the absolute nature.

The two aspects are like a duality of ultimate space and energy, whereas there really isn't any such thing as a duality since the two interpenetrate each other; the energy must come from somewhere (its source must be the ultimate space), and thus the two are inseparably one. Everything created is that original nature. Even "One" or "Oneness" is too much of an explanation since you cannot know It without a created mind, and hence there is nothing you can say at all.

If you really think about it, you might surmise that whatever stage sages provisionally identify as our "original nature" is also just another stage in an infinite sequence to the *real* ultimate root nature, and you would not be far off with such an assumption. But the level of Early (Primordial) Heavenly Qi is as far as they are willing to teach until you actually get that far in spiritual attainments. Basically, sages only want to speak of the first five highest stages of this matter. In other words, you have to develop five bodies composed of five different higher substances (essences) on the spiritual journey.

Most of the spiritual schools of the world specify both (1) ranks of attainment for the stages along the way to realizing the immediate source of the mind (called the Supra-Causal energy, universal *prana*, Later Heavenly Qi, clear light, uncreated light, universal illumination, substance of consciousness, cosmic consciousness, super consciousness, alaya consciousness, emptiness, etc.), and then (2) stages transcending those ranks heading towards the highest stage of becoming fully enlightened. The further you proceed at this task, which involves both wisdom and yoga, the higher your subsequent stage of spiritual progress and advancement.

It is very hard to reach the stage of enlightenment, and along the road of meditation and yogic practices required for this you will pass through many unusual things such as physical sensations, body transformations (the body will become warmer, softer and more flexible), profound mental experiences and the sequential attainment of other bodies that correspond to higher and higher ethereal, insubstantial, intangible, refined, supernal essences.

It is through these bodies that you possess superpowers such as being able to affect lower realms of matter or heal other people with the energies of higher levels. Perhaps this is hard to accept, but such powers and abilities have been amply demonstrated by many spiritual greats. However, sometimes even with those energies they cannot help you even though they desperately want to assist, and so sometimes they can do nothing at all to help people and their fates.

This is why you always have to take personal responsibility for your own life and take fate into your hands by becoming an active doer. Whenever adversity or unfortunate circumstances arise in life, you can become the force that creates a new and better fortune if you wisely take action to go against bad conditions. To move forward, you have to take responsibility for your life to progress against adversity or unfortunate circumstances.

Spiritual Practice

Now to reach realization of this self-nature requires much spiritual work and practice, and most people don't know how to do it. Their religion usually lacks sufficient teachings and so they must wait for the afterlife in which to fully and properly practice.

The only way to achieve enlightenment (both in Heaven and as a human) and the attainment of the corresponding *prana* body, is through tremendous training and a *regular system of practice that works on transforming both your mind and physical body to higher states of purity*. Along a proper path of spiritual practice, the more subtle essences within your body separate out via a slow purification process and you develop an independent life (body) composed of the next higher essence. This higher essence body resides within the shell of the lower body, but can come into and go out of the lower essence body at will. Thus it is free of the lower body constraints.

As we have seen with everything else, progress at these feats – because with each higher body you attain you must continue purifying it to produce a yet higher stage body that can enter and leave that one at will - is one of the major involvements on the road of spirituality. This is what religion is actually all about at the upper levels. It is not about the claims of Christianity, Judaism, Islam and so on. Spiritual progress – no matter what your religion or tradition - will require that you devote yourself to a system of consistent practice to be able to enter the stream for these heavenly accomplishments. You will therefore need a system of cultivation routines if you truly want to make genuine spiritual progress.

Usually those on the spiritual road, regardless of their religion, practice many different types of spiritual exercises. Ultimately they all involve cultivating your mind and the Qi of your body. The process of spiritual advance is therefore considered a sequence of purification stages affecting your mind, body (Qi) and behavior that must all be brought to a higher stage of purity. The trick to being successful at it is to use *several different spiritual cultivation methods* that are based on entirely different principles. This is the quickest way to reach higher realms of spiritual attainment.

The paramount spiritual cultivation technique that everyone must practice is the **meditation** practice of watching one's mind like an unbiased observer (vipassana). By practicing awareness that doesn't attach to thoughts, and which denies them that "attachment" energy, your thoughts will settle of themselves. When you refrain from adding energy to a process then it will naturally die down by itself, and so will your internal mental chatter. Your mind will empty of meandering thoughts naturally if you pay them no mind and it will eventually reach a profoundly quiet, empty mental realm of awareness due to meditation. This process of cultivation can be described as employing a "subtraction principle" to let thoughts naturally settle and disappear.

This is what you must practice to get to any higher stage of spiritual development regardless of your religion. The formula by which meditation works is therefore the principle of non-effort (just watching your thoughts with mental non-attachment), non-attachment while retaining awareness (instead of sleepiness or trying to block thoughts or restrain them) and the progressive elimination of untamed thoughts. As the monkey mind dies down because thoughts die down, this self-cultivation method is termed a subtraction process.

Another practice is that of continuously reciting a **mantra** which sets up vibratory forces within the body that transform it over time (opening up its Qi energy meridians along which vital energy flows); tires the mind to quell thoughts (leaving a realm of mental emptiness); and asks for assistance from higher powers who can lend their energies to your efforts.

Thus, mantra recitation works on quieting (emptying) and transforming your mind through different principles other than the subtraction process which empowers normal meditation methods such as vipassana. It also affects the Qi vital energy of your body. Mantras therefore require a mental tiring process, external assistance process, and vital energy process for their efficacy.

Visualization exercises are another type of spiritual practice that give your mind an extra burden in order to settle thoughts. They are based on an "addition principle" for quieting the mind. Visualization efforts (concentrating on creating mental images) tie up the mind's attention so that you ignore the passing of wandering thoughts that normally bother and obscure its pure essence (just as the ripples on the surface of a pond obscure the clear nature of its water).

Because random thoughts are ignored when your attention is devoted to producing and holding a visualized mental image, your mind will tie up distractions that normally obscure its clear nature (except for the mental image) as long as you remain focused, and when you release the image at the end of your session you can experience mental release, joy and emptiness. After a visualization session you let go of the constructed image you held in your mind and then can experience the pure nature of consciousness that is empty of thoughts.

Therefore concentrated visualization practice, which entails internally creating and then holding images in your mind without wavering, are a way to teach concentration and focus that will also help you settle your mind. Once again, the principle of using force to hold concentration, and thereafter letting go to experience a free mind empty of wandering thoughts, employs the adding principle of cultivation rather than the subtraction principle of watching thoughts and letting them die down. Putting it another way, visualization and meditation practice operate using entirely different principles.

The physical practice of **yoga** and the **martial arts** helps stretch both your muscles and the Qi channels within your muscles through which the vital energy in your body flows. They can also help activate your Qi vital energy that flows through these channels, and thus pave the way for creating a new internal subtle body composed of Qi – the first stage of the true spiritual path. Your Qi, or life force, is the energy that needs to become purified on the spiritual trail, which can only happen if it flows freely without obstruction to allow it to separate from the body, its lower nature. In spiritual practice, all lower essences eventually separate from the higher. A lower physical essence must become purified to produce an even higher essence. This is a process that occurs again and again as you generate several higher energy bodies until you reach the vital energy level that we call the *prana* responsible for consciousness and matter's creation. That Supra-Causal level of *prana*, or energy, is the Mother of all subsequent, denser stages of energy and matter.

As your vital energy begins to circulate more efficiently within your body due to the results of spiritual practices, the higher level vital energy can start to separate from its attachment to the body and take on an independent life of its own. This is why the internal alchemy processes this involves are termed a process of purification or *refinement*. The purifying transformations all follow the laws of nature. You just need to work hard at spiritual cultivation practice to produce them. **Pranayama** breath retention exercises, which use "forcing principles" to straighten and clear your body's Qi energy channels, are an example of the hard work you have to do.

When couples have **sexual intercourse** the internal energy (Qi) movements they feel inside their bodies, which are not due to nerve excitation, evidence the opening of energy channels in a different way than that which occurs through stretching or forceful pranayama practice. As long as one's internal energy is not lost during sexual activity (such as when a man ejaculates and feels spent because his energy leaves him), the flow of internal energy produced can help generate physical transformations that will ultimately help with the cultivation of clear consciousness. This progress in your Qi and energy channels is due to "vital energy principles."

Finally, when people practice acts of kindness, charity and compassion that involve sacrifice and service to others, the warm sensations they feel internally are due to the movements of Qi opening up energy channels in the heart area and other body regions. The **practice of goodness, wholesome deeds, virtuous ways and merit-making** can therefore play a role in improving the circulation of vital energy in the body. They can help you transform your Qi and Qi channels through the principle of "virtuous behavior."

When vital energy flows freely without obstruction within your body then consciousness can clear of wandering thoughts since thought arousal is connected with that flow of vital energy. Because your thoughts and vital energy are linked, in this way you can cultivate a higher stage of mental clarity and come closer to the experiencing higher spiritual states of consciousness.

These are just a few different types of cultivation practice that all lead to positive results but via different principles and mechanisms. If you want to increase your odds of success in spiritual progress, the best advice is to simultaneously practice a number of different exercises – such as meditation, mantra, visualization, pranayama, stretching, sexual conduct, virtuous ways, special diets, energy conservation - which all produce progress *based upon entirely different principles* as shown. All these methods are different, and yet they are all interconnected and all affect your Qi and channels.

The efforts required for the highest stages of spiritual achievement will be tremendous, and so *only a scheduled practice routine* - as we have previously seen in the cases of Liao Fan, Franklin, Bettger and with deliberate practice - will be sufficient to take you there. That schedule must employ multiple practices that involve different principles.

For instance, Zen master Changqing Huileng is said to have worn out seven meditation cushions in the course of practicing meditation.

Many masters have been recorded as saying they recited millions of mantras before achieving enlightenment.

Tibetan Lama Tsongkhapa is said to have generated ten million mandala offerings, which are complex mental visualizations you form in your mind during a state of mental stability.

Tirumalai Krishnamacharya, the father of modern yoga, assiduously practiced yoga for seven years studying 700 asanas from Ramamohana Brahmachari, who was a master himself of pranayama and 7,000 yoga asanas.

Ramakrishna of India practiced over several dozen and different specialized tantric practices for his spiritual cultivation, each of which involved different mental and energetic principles of transformation that affected his Qi and Qi channels.

Study is also important for spiritual attainment, and so during a three-year retreat Master Nan Huai-chin read through the entire Buddhist canon when it normally takes twenty years to do so.

To achieve the very highest stages of spiritual achievement, such extensive efforts are necessary. However, they are unlikely to be accomplished unless you employ a schedule of daily practice that involves cultivation methods of different types that *depend on entirely different mechanisms* for mind-body transformations. Entirely different principles are involved with the practices of mindful (awareness) meditation, mantra recitation, visualization practice, pranayama and yoga asanas or martial arts, virtuous merit along with performing good deeds, and sexual discipline.

You need a method to make spiritual progress. For instance, young David in the Bible was able to overcome the odds of beating Goliath because he had a method. If you are seeking spiritual progress then you can overcome the odds of not making progress by using a method, too. The best method is to simultaneously practice several different spiritual exercises, each of which works according to different principles, instead of relying on just one alone.

By simultaneously performing spiritual practices that work on different principles, according to a strict schedule like Liao Fan, Franklin, Bettger or that required by deep practice, you can finally achieve progress along the lines of spirituality even if you thought it wasn't possible. That is the simple truth to spiritual progress regardless of your path or religion.

Do you want to make progress along these lines and achieve a fate that is higher than simply going to heaven? Then toss the dice high to see how far you will get, for now you know how to spiritually practice.

Chapter 8
THE COMPOUNDING EFFECT FROM MAINTAINING CONSISTENT EFFORT

Malcolm Gladwell, who wrote the book *Outliers* about exceptional people who dominate their fields, makes the point that there is no secret to success. Whether it is Bill Gates, the Beatles, superstar athletes, Nobel scientists or famous explorers, successful people just put in more time than other people. Successful people do what the unsuccessful are unwilling to do, which is put in extra effort.

Bill Bonner put it this way, "Success is usually the product of compound effort over time. It takes time to develop contacts. It takes time to develop trust – both of your own team and outside clients/customers/associates. It takes time and experience to develop the hunches and instincts that are useful in real life. It takes time too to understand other people and learn how to work with them. It also takes time to build a foundation of human financial capital that allows you to take advantage of the insights and opportunities that experience bring you.

"Time does not work in a linear, mathematical way. As with compound interest, time pays off geometrically. As contacts, experience, wisdom innovations and intuition are added one to another, your opportunities multiply. A $100,000 deal that you might have done when you were 25 grows into a $1 million deal 5 years later. And instead of doing two deals a year, you might do 10 per year.

"This is also why it is important to put in lots of time. The leading figures in their industries put in thousands of hours – usually far more than their competitors. They may appear to be 'gifted.' Their achievements may seem effortless. But they are almost always the product of time.

"Not only that, but the time spent at the end is much more powerful than the time at the beginning. You can see this by looking at charts of compound interest. Starting from a low base, the first series of compound interest produce little difference. But at the end, the results are spectacular.

"Start with a penny. Double it every day. At the end of a week you are still only adding 32 cents per day. By the end of the third week, however, you're adding more than $10,000 per day. So you see, the last increments of time are much more important than the first. …

"Compound interest works because each addition is then put in service to earn another increment of gain. Compound effort works the same way Every insight, innovation and useful contact helps bring on another, bigger and better one. … The longer and harder you work at something, generally, the more success you have."[6]

Therefore, if you want to change your fortune and destiny, if you want to change your life, if you want to change your personality, if you want to achieve something of significance or defy fate, if you want to learn how to master some new skill, if you want to triumph over your genes, if you want to achieve some degree of eminence, if you want to achieve a degree of genuine spiritual progress

---

[6] Bill Bonner and Will Bonner, *Family Fortunes: How to Build Family Wealth and Hold on to It for 100 Years*, (New Jersey: John Wiley & Sons, 2012), pp. 146-148.

- it is all possible. You can do it. You can create a new life, fortune and destiny. You just need to make use of the principle of consistent compound effort.

How should you proceed? First, know exactly what you want. Visualize that picture in your mind. See things as you want them to be in your mind. Imagine that result in all its details and then think ahead, make a plan to achieve it and stick to it. Whatever you create in life will always be tied to your core human values and interests, so always examine your values to see that what you intend to produce is worthy of your time, energy, effort and life force. Life is short so make sure you spend your hours pursing what is important to you; rather than just letting things happen *make them happen*.

Always be flexible; adapt and change whenever necessary to achieve your goals but stay on track. Trust in the process and stick with it. The key to success in life is grit and perseverance until you succeed. You have to follow through on activities even in the face of difficulties.

As Robert Collier said, "Success is the sum of small efforts repeated day in and day out." Therefore, use the compounding of consistent effort to get to where you want to go.

Will the fact that you are making an effort guarantee success? In life nothing is guaranteed, but this is the course of action that works. You cannot guarantee the results of your efforts – just as you cannot control the results of your actions - but you can decide to take the chance of creation since fate is ultimately in your hands. If the results are worthwhile then make a move and take the chance.

Toss the dice high showing you are willing to take the risk, make the effort and achieve what you want.

Appendix 1
THE STORY OF SHAO KANGJIE

The story of the sage Shao Kangjie is a fascinating tale, and will help explain the origins of the Iron Abacus methodology.

Shao Kangjie, who is also known as Shao Yung or Shao Yong, was one of the five most famous Neo-Confucian philosophers during China's Sung dynasty. As a young man, though, he was always interested in numbers and symbols rather than philosophy and wanted to find some way to predict events in the world using calculations. He therefore studied the symbolism, numbers and transformations of the *I-Ching* under his teacher Li Zhicai, but could not yet find any way to use it to make predictions.

However, so ardent was he in his studies that he built himself a small hut in the woods where he could devote himself entirely to its contemplation. He pasted the walls and ceiling of the hut with the diagrams of the *I-Ching* so that wherever he might turn his head, sitting or lying down, he would see its hexagram symbols and could ponder how one hexagram could be transformed into another.

One day while studying in his hut he took a nap lying on a ceramic pillow. When he awoke he saw a rat in the hut scampering about and threw the pillow at it, which broke into pieces. He was surprised to find a piece of paper in the shards, which had been hidden inside the pillow. Written on the paper was a sentence, "In the year 1050 on April 10, in the afternoon, this pillow will be destroyed by being thrown at a rat."

This was the type of prediction Shao Kangjie had been trying to create, and he excitedly set out to see who wrote the message. Whoever wrote that piece of paper must truly know how to predict fate and might therefore have the formulas or other method he was seeking.

When he got to the shop owner who had sold him the pillow, the potter disavowed any knowledge of the paper, but said it might have been put there by a old man educated in the *I-Ching* who had once picked up the ceramic pillow and examined it. Together the two went off to his house to see if he was the one who had put it in the pillow.

Along the way to the old man's house they were met by his son who told them that their father had recently passed away, but that on this day a scholar would come looking for him and that he should be given a special book of *I-Ching* formulas he had written. "Through this book," the father had told him, "the scholar would be able to tell you how to get money for my burial."

Shao Kangjie took the book and went under a tree where he then spent some time reading it. After a while he made some calculations and told the family to dig under the northwest corner of the bed where they found some silver that their father had buried. This was exactly the money needed for his burial.

Within the book, which has been lost to history, were the original formulas Shao Kangjie had been seeking on how to use the *I-Ching* to calculate life cycles, fates and fortunes. Many fortune telling systems have been developed since that time, using those original formulas and others that Shao Kangjie developed and detailed in works like *Plum Blossom Numerology*. It is said that the Iron Abacus Numerology system was invented by Shao Kangjie or based upon his work.

Plum Blossom Numerology, written by Shao Kangjie, contains many details on how to calculate various fortunes. For instance, a particular story concerns one evening at 4 pm on the 17th day of the 12th month in the Chinese Year of the Dragon. Shao Kangjie was admiring the blossoms on a plum tree and saw two sparrows fighting in the tree. Suddenly, due to the fighting, they both fell to the ground.

Using the numerical calculation method explained in the book, Shao Kangjie used this event to predict that a young neighbor's girl would come to pick the plum blossoms and when threatened by the gardener, would fall from the tree and hurt her thigh. This is exactly what happened, and so this is why Shao Kangjie named the book *Plum Blossom Numerology*.

In another instance Shao Kangjie and his son heard a knock on their door on New Year's eve when a neighbor came to borrow something. Shao Kangjie asked his son to predict what it was, and through the principles of the book he predicted that it was something with a short metal head and long wooden handle. Therefore his son said it was a hoe. Shao Kangjie corrected him predicting it would be an axe, explaining "When you predict situations you have to use your knowledge and consider the time and situation. Since it's winter time and it's cold he would have no use for a hoe. Since on New Year's eve he would want to build a fire, naturally he would want an axe."

Shao Kangjie also once bought a lantern and calculated from his purchase that it would be broken at 12:00 noon on a certain day, month and year. Just before it was to be broken he put it on top of his desk and determined to watch it, curious to see how it would happen.

It was lunch time and his wife called him many times to come to eat, but he refused to acknowledge her because he was so intent on watching the fate of the lantern. Finally his wife came into the room and saw him staring at the lamp. In her anger for him ignoring her she took a broom and broke it. "So that's how it was to be broken," shouted Shao Kangjie ending the experiment.

As stated, many Asian fortune telling systems have been developed based on Shao Kangjie's initial teachings, including Iron Abacus Numerology. In this system, 24,000 sentences are written within 24 books where each line specifies an aspect of fortune such as "Your mom is thirty-four years older than you," "Your father will die in jail when you are nineteen years old," "You are the fourth son in the family," "Your father's occupation is that of a chef," "Your wife will be born in the Year of the Monkey," "You will have three children and the second will be a lawyer," "You will become a doctor," "You will move to a foreign land named ..." and so on.

Taking the year, month, date, hour and minute of your birth calculations are applied to these numbers using an algorithm that sequentially indicates forty or more indexed sentences that reveal a person's fortune.

Shao Kangjie explained many principles of fate prediction, but perhaps the most important was his advice "When there is no motion, no divination is possible. When nothing happens, one should not divine."

This extends to the principle of meditation for helping you change your fate, for when you can reach a state of mind which seems empty of thoughts or thought attachments, cultivating that state of pure awareness produces a freedom from following your karma which you can use to create a new fortune.

Appendix 2
USING BLOOD TEST "OPTIMAL REFERENCE RANGES" TO PICK YOUR NUTRITIONAL SUPPLEMENTS

Most people wisely believe that nutritional intervention might help with their various health conditions, but unfortunately don't know which vitamin/mineral or herbal supplements to use. Usually the scientific research presents them with a lengthy list of nutrient recommendations for a disease, but they are faced with supplement roulette since they don't know which items have the best chances to be the most effective.

As discussed, a knowledge of one's family tree can help in these situations because often you will see certain supplements commonly recommended for a large number of the conditions that plague a family. If a supplement consistently appears as a helpmate across the multiple conditions in your family, including the specific one you are concerned about, would it not be smart to consider what it might do for you?

A layman who triangulates the medical conditions on

his family tree with his own blood test indications can often determine the fewest items to try that might have the greatest impact or chances of assistance.

How do you tailor nutritional interventions more effectively and efficiently by examining your blood work? The most powerful book that can help you do this, and which should probably be in every home, is *Blood Chemistry and CBC Analysis* by Dicken Weatherby and Scott Ferguson (Bear Mountain Publishing, 2002).

This book easily enables you to determine if your blood markers are higher or lower than the *optimal ranges* for healthy people (not the wider "reference ranges" appearing on blood tests that are derived from population groups containing large numbers of sick people). It also explains what diseases you should suspect when your blood markers are "out of range." Furthermore, it also provides nutritional recommendations for returning things to normal.

For instance, if your blood work shows that your alkaline phosphatase levels are low, this suggests you are zinc deficient (which affects your taste buds and many biochemical processes within your body) and would physically benefit from zinc supplementation. The alkaline phosphatase enzymes depend upon zinc for their optimal functioning, so low Alk Phos levels suggest that there is not enough zinc in your system. If your fingernails have spots, your sense of taste has been declining or you suffer from acne, eczema, dry skin, thinning hair, or immune problems, these are all conditions that also suggest zinc deficiency in the body. Knowing these conditions and that you have a low zinc score based on optimal reference ranges, you would know to try using zinc supplements as a health assist since all these factors highlight it.

Low levels of SGOT/AST or SGPT/ALT or GGTP always suggest you might have a vitamin B-6 deficiency, which is useful information if vitamin B-6 keeps showing up as a recommended nutritional supplement for the health conditions in your family line.

If your LDH levels are high or uric acid levels are low, these are just a few of the many blood markers which can spotlight a vitamin B-12 or folate deficiency. These are easily obtained supplements commonly recommended for nervous system problems and mental illness (depression, autism, anxiety), cardiovascular disease (clogged arteries due to elevated homocysteine levels) and other problems.

A doctor once taught me that if your uric acid levels are less than 1.8 while total cholesterol is less than 140, triglycerides are less than 40 and lymphocytes are less than 20 simultaneously, then you better suspect cancer.

High chloride levels in conjunction with low CO_2 levels often indicate chemical sciatica, which is back pain that usually stumps the doctors since MRI, MEG and CT scans will be normal.

High creatinine levels often indicate the beginning of prostate problems while BUN can be used as a marker to indicate gluten sensitivity.

These are just a few examples of how optimal blood marker ranges can be used to identify hidden illnesses, or health conditions that have already manifested yet which puzzle the doctors. If you like watching detective shows on television then you might care to put on your detective's hat and spend an hour or so with a book like this and your own blood test (or those of a family member) to see what is awry, and then intervene. Like Caesar, risk to make the effort and transform your life!

When a lab report indicates that some of your test results are out of range, your healthcare provider should evaluate those results in the context of your medical history, your family's history, a physician's examination, and other factors. Unfortunately, healthcare providers don't have access to these optimal ranges, and so they often miss diagnoses that become simple with these ranges.

Many people have told me that in less than a hour they

were able to go through the optimal blood test tables and could diagnose family conditions that had stumped countless doctors. Even rare conditions that cannot usually be figured out will usually leave their tell tale traces in blood test markers that might only be spotted by knowing optimal blood chemistry ranges.

Blood Chemistry and CBC Analysis and other books (such as Jonathan Wright and Alan Gaby's *Nutritional Therapy in Medical Practice: Protocols and Supporting Information*, Melvyn Werbach and Jeffrey Moss's *Textbook of Nutritional Medicine*, and the Life Extension Foundation's *Disease Prevention and Treatment*) offer powerful lifestyle, dietary change and nutritional product protocols that can adventitiously be used to turn your health around. You can also find protocols at www.lef.org.

There are even books devoted to specific conditions such as Dean Ornish's books, and indicative titles such as *Prevent and Reverse Heart Disease: The Revolutionary, Scientifically Proven, Nutrition Based Cure* (Caldwell Esselstyn), *The End of Diabetes: The Eat to Live Plan to Prevent and Reverse Diabetes* (Joel Fuhrman), or *Dr. Neal Barnard's Program for Reversing Diabetes* (Neal Barnard).

The problem with the high and low reference ranges normally reported on blood tests, and the reason why they are less useful than "optimal ranges" reported in this book (in the table below) is that they are developed after measuring blood markers on a very large population of people, many of whom are sick and whose readings should therefore be excluded from use in determining what range should be "normal." Reference ranges are commonly constructed to cover 95% of the results for a population. "Normal" on these ranges therefore just means that you are not in the top 2.5% or bottom 2.5% of the population, which would be considered abnormal.

If the ranges reported were created from populations of entirely healthy people, which would make them much tighter, the violation of those ranges could serve as early warnings of dysfunctions and abnormalities before disease manifests in a full-blown state. That's why these optimal blood work ranges are far more useful than typical laboratory reference ranges. They can help you spot sub-clinical nutrient deficiencies that produce disease when doctors claim everything is normal.

In other words, when you receive your blood tests and the results still look normal – because you don't see any markers that violate the high or low ranges on the report - you can still be quite sick. There could still be a major dysfunction brewing that *might only be spotted by using the optimal rather than the average reference ranges*. So use the table below to help get you started. A test result outside of the optimal ranges listed may not necessarily indicate a problem, but it certainly signals you and your healthcare provider to investigate further. When you look up the meaning of a range violation in *Blood Chemistry and CBC Analysis*, you'll get an idea of possible health conditions to consider that you might be developing.

Because optimal blood ranges represent cut-off thresholds different than ordinary reference ranges, they can definitely help doctors *and you* spot dysfunctions and abnormalities before disease manifests. If you are therefore worried about the genetics in your family and fear you will develop a particular condition, these results can be your warning sign to *intervene now* and reverse a condition before it becomes more serious.

Optimal blood ranges can make blood work not just a prognostic tool but a *preventive tool* for seizing the day to change your life and become healthier, which is what this book is about. If you see blood test markers violating the "optimal" ranges and the explanations say that a range violation is indicative of a condition already in your family (that you attribute to "bad genes"), then it's probably time to intervene with systematic lifestyle, diet, nutritional supplement and other changes.

What are the optimal reference ranges and where did

they come from? Most of these ranges can trace their origins to those published and copyrighted by Harry Eidinier, Jr., Ph.D. in *Balancing Body Chemistry*. You can find similar "optimal" biomarker ranges offered by BodyBio.com and in the works of biochemist and physician Nick Abrishamian, Dr. Jack Tipps, Dr. R. M. Cessna, and others who all teach that "optimal ranges" can be used to spot conditions that might normally puzzle the doctors.

Here are the optimal ranges most commonly reported from their work, which can be found in table form in *Blood Chemistry and CBC Analysis:*

Glucose	80-100
HgB A1C	4.1-5.7%
BUN	10-16
Creatinine	0.8-1.1
Sodium	135-142
Potassium	4.0-4.5
Chloride	100-106
CO2	25-30
Anion Gap	7-12
Uric Acid	3.5-5.9 male; 3.0-5.5 female
Total Protein	6.9-7.4
Albumin	4.0-5.0
Calcium	9.2-10.0
Phosphorus	3.0-4.0
Gastrin	45-90
Alk Phosphatase	70-100
SGOT (AST)	10-30
SGPT (ALT)	10-30
LDH	140-200
Total Bilirubin	0.1-1.2 (>2.6)
Direct Bilirubin	0-0.2 (>0.8)
Indirect Bilirubin	0.1-1.0 (>1.8)
GGTP	10-30
CPK	30-180

Globulin	2.4-2.8
Alpha 1 Globulin	0.2-.3
Alpha 2 Globulin	0.6-.9
Beta Globulin	0.7-1.0
Gamma Globulin	1.0-1.5
A/G Ratio	1.4-2.1
Bun/Creatinine	10-16
Cholesterol	150-220
Triglycerides	70-110
LDL	<120
HDL	>55
Chol/HDL	<4
Total Iron	50-100
Ferritin	33-26 males; 10-122 female
TIBC	250-350
TSH	2.0-4.4
T-3 Uptake	27-37
T-3	100-230
T-4 Thyroxine	6-12
WBC	5.0-7.5
RBC	4.2-4.9 male; 3.9-4.5 female
Reticulocytes	0.5-1
Hemoglobin	14-15 male; 13.5-14.5 female
Hematocrit	40-48 male; 37-44 female
MCV	82-89.9
MCH	28-31.9
MCHC	32-35
Platelets	150,000-385,000
RDW	<13
Neutrophils	40-60%
Lymphocytes	24-44%
Monocytes	0-7%
Eosinophils	0-3%
Basophils	0-1%

ABOUT THE AUTHOR

Bill Bodri is the author of several business, investing, health and self-help books including:

- *Quick, Fast, Done: Simple Time Management Secrets from Some of History's Greatest Leaders*
- *How to Create a Million Dollar Unique Selling Proposition*
- *Breakthrough Strategies of Wall Street Traders: 17 Remarkable Traders Reveal Their Top Performing Investment Strategies*
- *Super Investing: 5 Proven Methods for Beating the Market and Retiring Rich*
- *High Yield Investments, Hard Assets and Asset Protection Strategies*
- *Super Cancer Fighters*
- *The Little Book of Meditation*
- *Visualization Power*

His how-to materials on how to change your investment fortunes are included in his book *Super Investing*, and his materials on how to change your entrepreneurial business fortunes are found in *How to Create a Million Dollar Unique Selling Proposition*.

The author can be contacted for interviews or speeches through wbodri@gmail.com.